PHILADELPHIA BOYHOOD

PHILADELPHIA BOYHOOD

GROWING UP
◆ IN THE ◆
1930s
▼

Paul Hogan

Holbrook & Kellogg ◆ Vienna, Virgina

Holbrook & Kellogg, Inc.
1964 Gallows Road, Suite 200
Vienna, Virginia 22182
(703) 506-0600

Cover Art: Jerry Litofsky
Layout and Graphic Design: Philip Dunn and Michelle Gilliam

Printed in the United States of America.

Philadelphia Boyhood: Growing Up in the 1930s
ISBN: 1-56726-027-6

Other books written by Paul Hogan—

Playgrounds for Free
The Nuts & Bolts of Playground Construction

For my Grandson, **Colin Paul Tareila**

Contents

Acknowledgments

My grandparents, parents, and siblings—Dan, Ed, John, and Jule—mentioned throughout the book clearly have been and still are the greatest influences in my life.

I want to acknowledge my neighborhood peers in the 1930s: Bobby Thompson, a grammar school buddy who is still a good friend; Eddie Armstrong, who taught me photography, still an important part of my life; Leroy Schoch, who taught me to play chess and think things through logically; Albert Orlando, who taught me to appreciate music, even his own coronet playing; Jack Conlin, who taught me the meaning of "street smart"; Ben Zimmerman, who taught me to love trains; Jack Paperman, who taught me to respect people; Howard Eisling, who loved animals and taught me to respect wildlife; Mr Frazier, who taught me respect for the military; The many Staceys and O'Conners, who filled our teams and games; Louise Leonard, who gave me birthday parties and comforted me when my mother died; Lucille and Dorothy Devlin, who helped me appreciate that girls could be pretty neat; Mike Bradley, who taught me to take a dare and win; Doc Bergman, who let me hang out at his drugstore and taught me how a business should be run; Joe Morris, who was my first friend to die in war.

Seeing this book into print has been a gratifying experience. I appreciate the support and help provided by Barbara Kres Beach, who has read it all and encouraged me through the editing process; my cousin, John Logue, retired professor from Villanova University, who has helped proof the manuscript and corrected historical references; George Brightbill, associate archivist of the Paley Library of Temple University, who reviewed and made thousands of photographs available to me. Finally, I want to thank Kathy Keenan, widow of my dear friend Arthur Keenan. Arthur and I served in World War II as paratroopers. Before he died, he asked me to take care of Kathy. I am.

Paul Hogan

Introduction

'Twas the season to be jolly and so we were. Each and every year my mother and I visited Santa Claus at Wanamaker's Department Store. We gazed with great wonder at the Christmas display windows and the wonderfully complicated Lionel train layouts complete with little villages, people, cars, and houses.

I remember when we were able to buy a quart of delicious Breyers Ice Cream at Bergman's Drug Store for just 50 cents. Doc Bergman would pack in so much ice cream that the lid was an inch off the top of the cardboard container—that much more for us to enjoy.

My trips to the Navy Yard with my brother Dan to visit his ship are forever etched in my memory. Eating Navy chow in the mahogany-appointed ward room with Dan and his crew and taking a nap in a real Navy bunk was an experience not every 14-year-old boy had.

For many of us, the Philadelphia we knew growing up is fading. As I write this, three of my favorite institutions are either closing or moving out of the city. After 130 years as the most prestigious department store in the nation, Wanamaker's has closed. Under its beautiful bronze eagle, millions of Philadelphians, including me, met their friends, family, and lovers. I treasure memories of attending Christmas concerts with my parents played on its magnificent organ.

Also closed is the Philadelphia Navy Yard, where I visited my brother Dan's ship before Pearl Harbor, and where I worked as a contractor after the Korean War. Things are ever changing. Breyers Ice Cream has closed, laying off workers who have been with the company for 30 years or more. Perhaps it's time to make my own ice cream again.

This book is a testimony to the gracious and loving people of Philadelphia—the folks who made Wanamakers, Breyers, and the Naval Shipyard great—and to the people and places I knew as a boy growing up in the Overbrook section of West Philadelphia in the 1930s. Although I was born in 1927, my vivid memories are of the 1930s and '40s. My childhood ended with Pearl Harbor. During 1941 and 1942 my life changed forever. My mother died, my father grew ill and was cared for by my sister, my three brothers went off to war, and I was packed off to boarding school.

Even when the lean years came, I don't remember being hungry, but I recall meals during which our family of seven shared a single quart of milk. As my brother Ed said recently, "We weren't poor. We just didn't have any money." We spread our toast with oleo, not butter, and my job was breaking and squeezing the tiny container of yellow dye inside the margarine package and kneading it until the lard-looking mass turned butter yellow.

But in earlier years, we had both an upstairs and downstairs maid, beautiful 17-year-old colleens who feather dusted and swept and kept us all in order. We had the only two-car garage on the block of houses my father built. In the 1920s, our family took elaborate vacations to Europe, which I don't remember because I wasn't born yet, but my father liked to remind me that I did travel with the family on our last grand vacation—by train West to California and then home via the Panama Canal—although I was in my mother's stomach at the time.

As the youngest child I was said to have grown up to be the spoiled one. I don't think I did. I earned my own money from the age of seven or eight. And I remember a stern lecture from my mother who upbraided me for spending a whole ten cents on a Big Little Book. Do you remember those small, thick books with an adventure comic on one page and the text opposite? Recently I paid $100 for a Buck Rogers Big Little Book, complete with a pop-up rocket. Today, of course, I wish I had bought more of these books as a child, and I wish I had saved them.

I had other passions on which to "squander" my hard-earned money. The three train sets I bought or traded, once valued at ten dollars or so, are now worth thousands. A pedal fire engine I enjoyed as a boy recently sold for $25,000 at Southebys in New York. But I didn't just covet things that cost money. We made our own toys and made up thousands of variations of our own games. We played Red Rover with dozens of neighborhood kids, and hockey on our concrete back alley without benefit of shoulder and knee protectors.

With the onset of the war, our play took a serious turn. As junior high schoolers, we carved model wooden planes to help soldiers and air raid wardens learn to identify both friendly and not-so-friendly plane silhouettes. I think I carved over a hundred. I collected aluminum pots and pans to help build fighter planes and bombers to shoot down Mitsubishis, tools of the former enemy who now peacefully invades our garages and homes.

Memories about growing up have been rattling around in my head like a loose sack of marbles for half a century. I thought it was time to give a few of them to my three children. Then, I thought, why not include my extended family—now over one hundred children, women, and men. And, finally but not least, I wanted to include you—neighbors and friends, familiar and unfamiliar, young and old—who share similar experiences and memories, who *remember* life in a designer-free environment or who *wonder* what it was like.

So is this a book of history? Sort of. Personal memories? Yes. A legacy for children, family, and friends? That, too. A love letter to everyone whose experience and memories weave the past into our present experience? Absolutely. Call *Philadelphia Boyhood* a love letter to you all.

Paul Hogan, Phoenixville, Pennsylvania, 1995.

How to Help Your Big Brother

Human reactions are paradoxical! I get angry when I drop a pencil and have to bend over to pick it up, or lose a few words from my computer. The more serious the incident the less angry I seem to get. So too with my big brother Ed.

I was thirteen years old. It was about 4:30 on a Friday afternoon in summer, 1940. I don't remember if it was Friday the Thirteenth, but it might as well have been.

My big brother Ed was in the shower getting spruced up for a heavy date. To quote from the song "Hey, Good-Lookin'," he had "a brand-new car [a 1940 Chevrolet] and a five-dollar bill." His rendez-vous wasn't "just over the hill," but in Washington, D.C., with his girlfriend who attended Catholic University.

After working all week as a carpenter Ed was running late, so I decided to help him on his way by getting his new car out of our garage. I got the keys and drove his car right through the garage wall into the basement laundry room! The grill was knocked in and the lights a bit askew. The crash would have totaled a 1995 automobile. I was ready to run away from home forever rather than face my big brother's wrath, but he came out before I had time to pack.

Ed just looked at the incredible damage to his new car, looked at me, sighed, got into his new wreck, and drove to his destiny in

Washington. He never said a word to me then or after about the crash. Of course, now, fifty years later, he berates me every chance he gets.

Forty years after I helped Ed, my thirteen-year-old stepson decided to help me when I was in a hurry to get somewhere by turning my brand-new pickup truck around, thus saving me a few seconds. He put it in gear and ploughed into a tree, creasing the whole right side.

He was terror-stricken when I rushed out of the house and saw the damage. I was prepared to kill him. Then my memory went into fast reverse and I remembered my brother's non-reaction to my crime. I just laughed, got in the truck, and drove off leaving my stepson bewildered. I didn't tell him for several years of my similar crime when I was exactly his age.

What goes around comes around.

Cape May

Our cousins, the Logues, had a great big summer house in Cape May, New Jersey, just three blocks from the ocean. Every summer, some or all of us five Hogan kids would visit the five Logue kids for a week or more. My older siblings often went by themselves, but I was only five or six and was always accompanied by my mother. My father rarely if ever went, because he was either working or feuding with my Uncle Ed.

My mother and I would take the Number 41 trolley car to the Market Street Elevated and get off at the Ferry Terminal Station at Delaware Avenue and Walnut Street. We paid our nickel and rode the ferry to Camden, New Jersey, where we transferred to the Reading Railroad steam train to Cape May. We made the trip in less time then than it takes now on the freeways.

The train ride was over too soon. We were met at the Cape May station by a horse and carriage for the short ride to my cousins' house at 1023 Maryland Avenue. Perhaps the horse and carriage was a figment of my imagination, as my older cousin, Frank Logue, swears there was no horse and carriage. I'll leave it in, as it adds a little more romance to the memory.

The house was three stories and could easily accommodate the ten kids, four adults, two maids, a cook plus an extra guest or two. It was at the end of Maryland Avenue, next to a large meadow of salt hay. At the other end of the meadow, perhaps a half mile away, was the

*The Logue's Maryland Avenue house at Cape May in 1994.
Little has changed since 1934.*

*The Hogans & Logues at Cape May. Mother, Dan, Ed, John, Jule, Ellen
Logue, me, Frank, John, Gordon and Ed Logue and Aunt Rene.*

dirigible hangar at the Cape May Naval Air Station—now a Coast Guard training station.

There was a narrow rutted dirt road from my cousins' house to the air station. After a rain I would run out and dam up the ruts in an intricate spillway system with sluices and gates. At first I used sticks for boats but one of my brothers or cousins fashioned little boats made from pieces of lath. Some even had small sails. I would construct all sorts of structures until the water drained away or evaporated. I guess that was the beginning of my career in construction. I never saw a vehicle on my private road. Going back in the summer of 1994, I discovered my private dirt lane was now a black top street with houses as far as the eye could see. There is no dirigible hangar there now.

Almost every morning my mother would take me for a walk along the beach. We started out very early. I remember seeing the sun come up, but I guess it was a bit later. Along the way, we beachcombed. From my mother I got my lifelong hobby of scavenging. Forgetful kids and the morning tide would leave toy wooden boats, burned out light bulbs, and beach balls stranded high and dry on the beach—all sorts of interesting flotsam and jetsam were delivered right to my feet by the pounding waves.

After collecting the day's loot, I would spend many happy hours constructing sand castles and raceways for the tennis balls I'd found. The castles had roadways, bridges, and tunnels on and through which I'd send the balls down scores of times before the tide would come in and return my castles to their previous state.

While I remember making that dawn walk with my mother a hundred times, most probably it was just

The beachcomber in 1929—Cape May.

once or twice. Such is the impression of happy youthful experiences.

On April 4, 1933, the mighty U.S. Navy dirigible *Akron* crashed in the Atlantic Ocean just off the Jersey coast. With 73 sailors killed, it was, at that time, the worst air disaster in history. The school year had not yet ended, so we were not near the shore. Navy salvage crews brought a great deal of the wreckage to the dirigible hangar at Cape May, just up the dirt road from my cousins' summer house.

My brother Ed was always hanging around the hangar and had made friends with many of the sailors stationed there. When we got to Cape May, most of the pieces from the *Akron* were lying on the hangar floor while the investigators tried to figure out why the great airship crashed. A sailor friend of my brother's gave him an aluminum strut that didn't seem to fit into the puzzle. The section was about two by three feet, with several lighter cross-angle struts to give it extra strength, and weighed less than a pound. It hung on Ed's bedroom wall until he went off to war. Then, like almost everything else from our childhood, the relic disappeared.

Ed also saw the German DO X flying boat up close. The DO X was the biggest airplane ever built up to that time. It had twelve engines on top of the upper biplane wing. There were six engine mounts and each mount held both a pusher and puller engine with huge propellers.

The DO X was on its way to South America and was following the shoreline about fifteen feet above the water and only a few hundred yards off shore. I suppose the pilot was taking advantage of the "ground effect phenomenon." When a plane flies very close to the ground or water the air is compressed between the ground and the wing and thus gives the plane extra lift.

Ed swears that as the giant seaplane flew by, a crewman, who looked like a cook, was standing in an open door and waved to him. The plane had no more air speed than a fast train, and if train cooks can stand in a door and wave, I guess airplane cooks can too.

The DO X carried over 145 passengers and a crew of more than a dozen. There were beds and easy chairs, a kitchen, and a smoking lounge, and it was probably more comfortable than being jammed into today's 747 with 450 other weary travelers.

The one unpleasant chore I had every day in Cape May was a noontime spelling lesson. I could never learn how to spell wagon, even though my most treasured possession was a little red wagon. I either

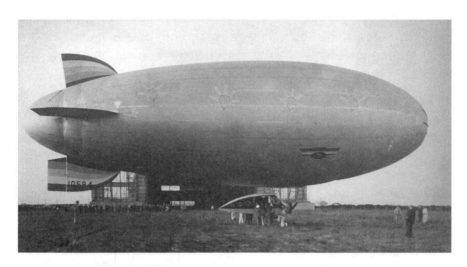

A Navy Blimp outside the Cape May Naval Air Station in the 30s.

The Dornier DO X, a German flying boat.

had to learn how to spell or repeat first grade. My mother, a former schoolteacher, was not about to have her youngest child held back.

As the Depression deepened, my Uncle Ed died, the Logue houses in Philadelphia and Cape May were sold, and my Aunt Rene and her five children moved to Overbrook in West Philadelphia, just three blocks from our home.

Envelope commemorating the first DO X landing in the US. 1931.

The Trip Not Taken

A few years ago, over a Memorial Day weekend, I visited my daughter Paula in Maine and my two-and-a-half-year old grandson Colin. When it was time to leave for the airport, Colin began to cry. He stood by the door and couldn't believe I was leaving him.

"OK," my daughter said to Colin, "you can go to the airport with Grandpa, but you must come back home with your grandmother." While utter joy overcame Colin, a bitter memory overcame me. We made the hour and a half drive to Bangor and Colin was sleeping contentedly when we arrived. He stirred slightly as I kissed him.

Sixty years before, when I was Colin's age, my cousins came by our house before leaving on their annual trip to Cape May. Like Colin, I wailed to go with them and even got into their car and tried to hide behind my cousins in the back seat. My mother said I couldn't go, but I refused to get out of the car. Finally, she gave in and said, "Well, if you're going to be away for such a long time, at least give me a kiss good-bye."

I jumped from the car and was swooped into her arms for a good-bye kiss. My cousins drove away.

My mother, Julia Cecilia Fay Hogan. About 1908.

My Mother

My mother, Julia Cecilia Fay, was born on June 12, 1889, in Philadelphia, the daughter of Ellen and Edward Fay. She attended the Philadelphia Girls High School and the Philadelphia Normal School, graduating in 1907 with a certificate allowing her to teach school. She did two years of postgraduate work at the University of Pennsylvania.

I found this 1902 postcard of my mother's alma mater in a Seattle used book store last year.

She married my father, Daniel E. Hogan, already a successful builder, on November 25, 1915. They first lived at around 53rd and Westminster in West Philadelphia. In 1917, my father built forty-five row houses on the 6000 block of Columbia Avenue, and my parents, with my oldest brother, Daniel, moved into one of the row houses on the odd side of the block while finishing construction of our final home on the corner of 61st and Columbia Avenue. That house, 6044, was the highest house in West Philadelphia. All the other houses had two floors; ours had three. Our house was built on two building lots, not one.

I remember just a few really happy years from around three years to six or seven years of age when my mother enjoyed good health and had a robust outlook on life. She was far more liberated in those days than most of her female contemporaries. She had her own car, and was always shopping, visiting friends, or going to art galleries. Our trips to the Italian Market on 9th Street in downtown Philadelphia stay in my memory as do many other buying forays to the city. We had a maid and a cook so my mother was free to come and go as she pleased. My parents made several trips to Europe and California by way of the Panama Canal before I was born.

Just when I started to become an individual personality at age seven, my mother took sick with a variety of problems, including a weak heart. Most of my recollections from then on were of her being sick in bed. I sometimes waited on her, bringing tea or a newspaper or getting the phone so she could call her sister, my Aunt Rene.

I remember most of the holidays, Thanksgiving especially, when we had our cousins, the five Logue children, and Aunt Rene over for a wonderful turkey dinner. Mother sang and played the piano and acted in our family puppet shows. She subscribed to *Etude* magazine and often played new musical scores she found in it. She was cultured, and regularly attended the Philadelphia Opera with my father, where we had a box for years. I never went.

While she didn't die until November 17, 1941, when I was fourteen, I felt that she had long been far from me as a mother. I knew she loved me as I loved her, but she just wasn't there most of the time. I'm sure had she had better medical care and the miracle drugs of today, she would have been with us a longer time and that time would have been more healthful, what we now call "quality time."

Mother, Jule, Dan, Ed & John. 1925.

The Italian market on 9th Street in Philadelphia in 1951.

Because Jule and I were both in school, her illness was especially difficult for us. Jule was more often absent than present during our mother's final year, having to nurse her daily. One or two of her teachers gave Jule understanding words of sympathy. But from the rest, she got mostly verbal abuse for her absences. I wonder if today's teachers are more tuned in to their charges' personal family problems than ours were. I hope so.

My mother did teach me correct table manners and how to speak the King's English with kind corrections when I erred. One lesson in manners stands out. My brother Ed had the habit of coming to dinner in his underwear. No amount of chastisement from my mother seemed to have an effect, until one memorable evening when my brother had a friend over for dinner. My mother appeared half in rags and half in underwear. She sat at the table and calmly served the food to Ed's everlasting embarrassment. Ed always dressed properly for dinner after that. That was a great lesson for me and I used it in varied ways on my own children when reason and threats wouldn't work.

I never visited my mother's grave until a few years ago when we buried my brother Dan next to her, my father, and my grandparents.

The Queen Mary and the Normandie

We had the only two-car garage on the block. It rarely had a car in it, so it usually served as a clubhouse, a stall for my brother John's pony, or a swimming pool in the summer. The floor was about two feet below ground level and there was a concrete ramp down into the garage much like a boat launch at a lake. My father had waterproofed the back wall so that when it was flooded the water wouldn't go into our basement behind the garage, even though the depth of the water was two feet.

During the 1930s we were fascinated by the great ocean liners, much as kids today are involved with the space shuttle and lunar landers. We knew all about the huge liners that raced back and forth across the Atlantic to win the coveted Atlantic Blue Ribbon for the fastest voyage between Europe and New York. All of us had models of the *Queen Mary,* the *Normandie,* the *Bremen,* or the *George Washington.*

Once my brother Ed decided to make a floating model of the *Queen Mary* large enough to carry him. He got plans of the real ship and scaled them down to a hundred to one. As the *Queen Mary* was approximately one thousand feet long, his model would be nearly ten feet long.

Almost every night for a month, Ed worked in our basement workshop, sawing, gluing, bending, tacking canvas on the ribs and painting. He was very thorough, even as a young teenager, and we eagerly watched his progress as the pint-sized *Queen Mary* took form.

I was too young to understand how technical and difficult his work was, but I was content to sit on a box and watch him labor over his masterpiece.

Many of the children on our block came every evening to watch him work. Our garage never looked so clean. The bikes, wagons, and horse stall were removed in preparation for the launch. The only structure not removed was a little hut my father had built for me on the large tool shelf over where the hood of the car would normally be. Ed knew better than to mess with my hut.

The launch date was set for a Saturday morning. The event was a major item in our block newspaper, and just about every kid in the neighborhood made plans to come to the garage to participate in the launching of the ships in the "swimming pool."

After school on the Friday before launch day, my brother John decided that he too would build a boat. He named his after the beautiful French liner, the *Normandie*. Unlike Ed, John didn't bother with plans, specifications, and detail drawings. John just gathered the leftover wood and canvas from the *Queen Mary* and made a kind of kayak about eight or nine feet long, one one-hundredth the size of the original.

Some of the kids laughed at John's feeble attempt to imitate his older brother. Others wisely kept their opinions to themselves. John worked until after midnight applying the last coats of paint to the canvas covering. He went to bed very tired. Happiness, success, and anticipation accompanied him to sleep.

Ed insisted that the launch take place exactly at 10 A.M., not a minute before or after. After all, they didn't wait around to launch real ships until a crowd arrived at the shipyard. Even so, most of the kids on our block were waiting long before the appointed time.

My sister Jule was disappointed when she wasn't chosen to christen the boat by pouring a bottle of water over the bow. Ed had his eye on a new girl in the neighborhood and gave her the honor. In the background, John had dragged his *Normandie* into position just behind the *Queen Mary*.

At exactly ten o'clock, Ed blew a whistle, his new girlfriend poured the water on the bow, and the *Queen Mary* was pushed into the two-foot-deep garage pool. Just as it got free of the garage ramp, Ed jumped in and began to paddle with his homemade oars. The *Queen Mary* immediately capsized, dumping Ed into the icy water.

While everyone witnessed this tragedy at sea, John quietly launched his *Normandie,* got in, and paddled over to Ed. John reached out his hand and said, "Do you need any help?"

The Queen Mary and the Normandie docked together in New York. 1939.

My Father, Daniel Edward Hogan. 1900.

My Father

My father, Daniel E. Hogan, one of eleven children, four of whom survived childhood, was born in Philadelphia on May 29, 1879. He attended Catholic school until the third grade, then transferred to the public school system. On graduating from the eighth grade around 1893, he worked, as most boys did in those days, running errands and helping older men in the construction field by carrying water, bricks, etc.

While in his late teens, he got a job as a reporter for the now extinct *Philadelphia Telegraph*. His beat was in the coal regions and he told me stories of his escapades. He was a great raconteur. Although he traveled a lot for his paper he managed to attend Drexel University night school where he studied English and writing. While making his newspaper rounds in the Pennsylvania coal region, he would stop at dentists' offices and buy the gold removed from pulled teeth. That gold horde provided the bankroll for his new building business.

One newspaper joke he told me was of a reporter named Flanagan whose volubility in his telegraphed news items far exceeded the paper's budget. After several admonishments he resolved to reform. Sent out to cover a train wreck, he wired his editor, "Off again, on again, Flanagan."

Another story he liked to tell about his days as a reporter concerned his teeth. They were always in perfect condition and the coal miners he dealt with always complimented him on his beautiful set of false teeth. He used to smile and tell his friends that he paid just $5 for them.

My father. 1930.

My Father and I at Jule's wedding. August 1944.

His listeners marveled at the bargain, never knowing that my father had his own beautiful teeth.

A century ago, he was one of the few young men in the city of Philadelphia who could swim the Australian Crawl. In addition to attending Drexel, he also took swimming lessons, something almost unheard of in the nineteenth century. He married my mother, Julia Cecilia Fay, in 1915.

Father was a very successful contractor and built more than a thousand houses around Philadelphia, Delaware, and New Jersey. When I was no more than five, he would often take me to work with him and I enjoyed playing in the sand pile, collecting pieces of wood, and salvaging both bent and straight nails the carpenters dropped. My pay was one cent for twenty straight nails or fifty bent ones. I remember the two-bedroom houses he built in Runnemede and Mt. Ephraim, New Jersey, in 1941. He sold them for $3,400. Last year, I charged that much to construct a child's backyard tree house.

One Sunday evening in 1929 he received a phone call from a friend who advised him to take all his savings out of one of the banks he dealt with. One version of the story has it that the caller was my Uncle Ed Fay, but due to a feud, he ignored the advice. In any case, he went to the bank at six the next morning only to find a line of anxious depositors circling the block. The bank never opened, and he lost $50,000 in bank stock. If you had $50,000 in bank stock, you lost that plus another $50,000. Lord knows what that would be in 1994 dollars—close to one million, I'm sure.

By the time he was in his late fifties, the burdens placed on my father during a lifetime of hard, productive work, taking care of a wife, five children, a mother-in-law, and various hangers-on, had grown too much for him. Among the harder blows were the bank failures, the Depression, losing ownership of our house, and the fact that my father had no work for a long time. He suffered a nervous breakdown from which he never really recovered.

There were many good memories of my father. Once, a new family moved into a house across and down the alley from us. For some minor infraction, the new neighbor gave me a hard slap. When my father heard about it, he marched right into the man's kitchen and gave him a harder slap. My father was then in his sixties and the other guy was in his thirties!

Most of my adolescent years I remember him just sitting on the end of a wicker sofa on our front porch, looking out the window, probably seeing nothing. I came and went as I pleased because my mother was also very sick and unable to keep me reined in. That task was left to my sister Jule, just three years older than myself.

When I was seven or eight, I took on the household duties of a teenager. I mowed the lawn and trimmed the hedges because there was no one else around to do it and the house was falling into shambles. By ten, I was climbing ladders and changing the screens for storm windows and vice versa every spring and fall. It wasn't all fun and games.

Around the time my mother died in 1941, my father rallied a bit and managed to persuade a bank to underwrite two houses he wanted to build on property he owned in Audubon, New Jersey. He never finished, and the bank began calling every day. One morning, the loan officer was waiting for my sister Jule, then about sixteen, as she was on her way to school. She had a night job on the Pennsylvania Railroad and was perpetually tired. The loan officer told my sister, "If the houses aren't completed, we will foreclose and we will have to take every stick of furniture you have."

The loan officer and my sister went over to Audubon and together developed a plan to complete the houses. Jule hired carpenters and plasterers, painters and plumbers, and finished the houses. With going to school during the day and working for the railroad at night, she still found time to take three buses to Audubon every few days to check on the workmen. The bank paid the workmen and the

My father. 1941

My father and Jule. 1930.

houses were finally sold. We didn't get anything, but we didn't lose what little we had left either.

Ironically, my brother Dan, then newly married and a first lieutenant in the Navy with a nice, almost new, used car, later wrote that 1941 was the happiest, most carefree year of his life. For my sister Jule, it was the meanest, most heart-rending year. She had tended my mother every day for years until the day my mother died. Jule had to contend with my irascible father and see that the electric bill was paid and that coal was in the bin—things a eighteen-year-old girl should not have to experience.

My father ended up in a series of nursing homes, paid for by my brothers Dan and Ed. Sometimes he'd walk off and the police would bring him back. At the time my brother John was killed in 1953, he had suffered a heart attack and wasn't expected to live. We didn't tell him of John's death. When he recovered, the family decided to continue the subterfuge. I was appointed to write to my father in John's name as though he were still living. That painful charade continued until Dad died in 1961 at the age of eighty-two.

6044 Columbia Avenue before World War II.

Home Movies for Fun and Profit

The first movie I ever saw was *The Phantom of the Opera,* starring Lon Chaney. I was about five, and the theater was in our basement at 6044 Columbia Avenue in West Philadelphia.

Ed and Dan, my two eldest brothers, decided to go into the movie business one summer to make money. They bought a used 16mm movie projector somewhere, made an electric movie sign, rented a film, and were in business. Well, it wasn't quite that simple.

After they got the projector, they had to build the theater. Our basement was ideal. It had an outside entrance into a laundry room, then a long hall into the main part of the basement. Our father had built our house on a double lot. The front room of the basement was about twenty-five by twenty feet and could comfortably hold thirty or forty kids. They got several old chairs and built benches from two-by-ten boards set on top of wooden milk crates.

Next came the theater sign, which they made from cutting out the letters M-O-V-I-E from a cardboard shoe box and fitting it up with a fifty-watt bulb. Then came the advertising campaign, which was accomplished by making duplicate copies of the program and typing the film notices onto some sort of gelatinous material which could transfer ink from a roller onto the page. The adverts were then hand delivered and nailed on utility poles in the neighborhood.

The movies always started at 10 A.M. My brothers couldn't begin to compete with the Saturday afternoon matinee at the Hamilton Theater. Admission was ten cents.

On Friday afternoon, my father drove into the city to rent the films. Meanwhile, my mother went to the Italian Market and bought several boxes of penny candy. On Friday night my brothers set up the benches and the movie projector behind a plywood partition and had a private viewing of the next day's feature.

My mother and father added to the store-bought selection by making their own wonderful homemade candy. The best candy I have ever tasted then or now was a concoction created by my father that he called Cola Cashew. It was a chewy, toffee-like candy with a cola flavor and cashew nuts added. I still think it would be a great commercial success. The candy stand was set up just after the admission counter at the cellar doorway.

I was only five so had no job other than to try to steal candy when no one was looking.

Opening day was a huge success with over forty children lined up to buy tickets. Besides the main feature there were a few short subjects such as *Felix the Cat.* I, of course, got in free. My brothers had only one projector so there were several intermissions while they changed reels. They made sure the intermissions were long enough for the kids to go to the bathroom and buy more candy from Jule and my mother.

The movie season lasted all summer long. I guess that's where I developed my love for movies, and I still go several times a month. But I have yet to taste candy as good as Cola Cashew, and I haven't seen a movie since that premier cinema performance that compares with Lon Chaney in *The Phantom of the Opera.*

The Hindenburg

The 6000 block of Columbia Avenue in West Philadelphia is exactly 408 feet long. I know because I measured it one day in the 1930s, using my father's 100-foot tape. There are twenty-three houses on the even side of the street, and twenty-four on the odd side. I know because my father built all of the houses, keeping two lots for our corner house at 61st Street.

We enjoyed other distinctions. Our house had three stories while all the others had only two. Thus when we climbed out the third floor rear bedroom window, we could walk over the other rooftops as far as 60th Street. Regrettably, all the bathroom skylights had frosted glass.

One summer day in 1936 the *Hindenburg* flew right over our block. I knew a lot about the zeppelin. I knew that it was 804 feet long, a few feet shy of being twice as long as our block of forty-seven houses. The *Hindenburg* was 150 feet in diameter, just about the width of our block. We saw the great airship late in the afternoon. A dull roar in the distance, sounding like far-off thunder on a summer evening, announced its arrival.

We had heard that the *Hindenburg* was ahead of schedule. We kids were eagerly awaiting it, hoping that it might fly over Philadelphia. Often, when the *Hindenburg* arrived ahead of its scheduled pre-dusk landings at Lakehurst Naval Air Station, when there was little wind to hamper the difficult mooring tasks, it would fly over New York or Philadelphia to "show its flags."

The Hindenburg flying over Lancaster Avenue in West Philadelphia in the summer of 1936. Notice the two-block shadow over Powelton Village.

The flags were gigantic swastikas painted on the huge tail fins. Each crooked cross was at least fifty feet square. I wasn't aware of what the swastika meant. I was only nine years old. I did know that the huge five-colored intertwined rings painted on each side of the dirigible commemorated the Olympic Games being held that year in Germany. In those days both the winter and summer games were held in the same country. Germany had them both in 1936. The summer games were held in Berlin and the winter games were held in Bavaria.

As soon as we heard the noise in the distance, several of my friends and I ran up to the roof of our house so we could view the airship unimpeded by trees or houses. As the sound grew louder we looked down and watched our neighbors come out of their houses to stare up into the sky with us.

Within minutes we saw the huge craft head right for our neighborhood. Directly overhead, it eclipsed the sun, covering two whole city blocks with its noisy shadow.

It couldn't have been more than just a few hundred feet over our heads. It certainly was less than our 408-foot block from us. We looked up and saw many passengers leaning out the window waving to us as they slowly drifted over us. We kids waved and cheered as the ship continued toward City Hall over Lancaster Avenue. When it reached the statue of William Penn astride City Hall, 535 feet above the ground, it circled once and then headed for its landing rendezvous at Lakehurst.

When the *Hindenburg* finally disappeared, we spent the rest of the day wondering what it must be like to pilot a great airship across the Atlantic in just two and a half days. We agreed that the size and comfort of the *Hindenburg* were all but unimaginable. Still, we had seen it with our own eyes. We had to imagine the inside of the airship from photographs and newspaper articles. The ship carried an aluminum grand piano that weighed less than 350 pounds. There was a dining room, a lounge, a fifty-foot long promenade deck, twenty-five staterooms, and a machine capable of distilling drinking water from the atmosphere. All of that just floated along like a wind-driven cloud filled with people.

The *Hindenburg* didn't fly over the Atlantic during the winter as the winds were too strong and too erratic. We looked forward to spring 1937, when we might again see the *Hindenburg* fly over West Philadelphia. It left Germany on the evening of May 3, 1937, and headed

Courtesy of the Luftschiffbau Zeppelin Museum, Friedrichshafen.

The lounge of the Hindenburg.

directly for Lakehurst, New Jersey. We listened to the radio each morning and night to learn its position and estimated time of arrival. We hoped it would be ahead of schedule and fly over our block again. It was not to be. There were strong headwinds and the *Hindenburg* was late. Even as dusk fell, gusts hampered its mooring.

We gathered around the radio and learned that it would tie up about 7:30 that evening, May 6. We anticipated the landing almost as much as children anticipated the moon landing thirty-two years later. We heard the announcer, Herb Morrison: "Here it comes ladies and gentlemen, and what a sight it is, a thrilling one, a marvelous sight. It is coming out of the sky pointing toward us, and toward the mooring mast. The mighty diesel motors roar, the propellers biting into the air. No one wonders that this great floating palace can travel through the air at such a speed with those powerful motors behind it."

We looked at each other. We knew the man on the radio was talking about the same things we had seen the summer before. But on May 6, 1937, at 7:25 P.M., we heard the announcer's voice change from wonder to panic. "It's burning, bursting into flames, and it's falling on the mooring mast and all the folks. Oh, the humanity and all the passengers!"

We were stunned. We couldn't speak for several minutes. We just listened to the announcer describe the burning skeleton and people running from the inferno.

My parents, knowing how horrified we kids were after hearing first-hand of the tragedy, let me go out and meet my friends, and we talked for hours about the crash. We sensed that this was the last crash of a lighter-than-air ship. Despite the great feats of the *Graf Zeppelin* and the U.S. Navy's only remaining dirigible, the *Los Angeles,* we knew that with the crashes of the *Shenandoah, Macon,* and *Akron*, and now the *Hindenburg*, there would never be another big airship built like those, and we would never be dirigible pilots.

We wondered what would happen to the *Hindenburg*'s sister ship, the *Graf Zeppelin.* Would it continue to fly to Rio de Janeiro from its base in Wilhelmshaven, Germany, or would the Germans just give up? A few weeks later we learned that the *Graf Zeppelin* was ordered home from Rio, never to make commercial flights again. It was dismantled and in 1941 its scrap aluminum was given over to the German war machine.

For weeks we read the papers and watched the newsreels of the crash at the Hamilton Movie Theater, a few blocks from our house. It was the first real tragedy I had ever experienced so closely. I was devastated and heartbroken as only a ten-year-old could be. I don't think I experienced anything like it until the *Challenger* went down. But the *Challenger* didn't fly over my house, and the astronauts didn't wave to me as they passed by.

Later, during the war, we saw dozens of blimps on training missions fly over our house. They were stationed at Lakehurst and the crews sometimes got a little off course from their antisubmarine exercises. My sister Jule had a boy friend who was learning to command a blimp. One day, he got off course and found himself and his crew over our house. He dropped a dozen eggs in our backyard for bombing practice. When his commander heard of the prank, his first assignment was to a remote duty station in Brazil to hunt for U-boats in the South Atlantic. I never saw him again.

Still later, in 1946, I met Maria Kleeman, who had survived the crash of the *Hindenburg.* Let me explain. My brother Dan married Gisela Bolton, the granddaughter of Frau Kleeman. Gisela's mother had become seriously ill and her grandmother came to the United States to visit her daughter on the *Hindenburg.* The fastest steamship from Bremen would have taken over a week. Frau Kleeman chose to fly and as a result had a part in one of the greatest air disasters of all time.

Gi's father was waiting at the Lakehurst Naval Air Station to take his mother-in-law to the hospital to visit her daughter. He saw the crash and could not imagine that Frau Kleeman would be one of the 61 survivors. It wasn't until the next day that he found her and learned that a crewman had grabbed her and run away from the exploding hydrogen. She suffered only a few slight burns, and was released from the hospital on May 7.

Maria Kleeman, left, a few weeks after escaping from the burning Hindenburg, with her daughter Katherine Bolton, my brother Dan's mother-in-law.

I met Frau Kleeman several times in the late forties, when, after the war, she came to spend her final days with her daughter. She was a bit reluctant to talk about the crash but said she was just looking out the window at the landing activities when the ship blew up. She told me she remembered nothing until she was released by the crewman a few hundred yards from the mass of molten metal.

Years later when I owned my own construction company, I won a contract to convert part of the dirigible hangar at Lakehurst into a helicopter maintenance school. I often brought along my small son, Teig, as my father had brought me along on his jobs. Inside the hangar a blimp was moored next to the balcony where I was working. Several times we visited on board the blimp, and my son took his afternoon naps in one of the bunks the crew used during long flights.

Now, whenever I travel to Washington, I visit the Air and Space Museum. I head right for the *Hindenburg* exhibit and stand at the window to look through at the dining room place setting: half a dozen crystal glasses for as many wines, five gold-rimmed plates, and a dozen pieces of monogrammed silverware are in place. A light beige napkin is folded in the middle of the top plate, and next to the right-hand silver is a beautifully printed menu. I close my eyes and sit down. The waiter pours the first of the wines and opens the menu for me. As I lay my napkin on my lap, I look out the large window at the Atlantic 5,000 feet below. I catch a glimpse of the *Queen Mary* racing after the *Normandie,* heading in the opposite direction. In a moment, the great ocean liners are lost in the distance. The sun sets. I turn from the window, toast my companion, and begin dinner.

Mother and Dan in Venice. 1925.

My Brother Dan

Dan was born in 1917, the same year as President Kennedy. If any of us can be said to have been born with a silver spoon in his mouth, I guess Dan would be the one. He grew up in a family with two maids, two cars, two houses (one summer shore house in Ventnor, New Jersey), and made a few trips to Europe with my wealthy parents, all this before the Great Depression, which hurt our family so badly.

In his early teens he was a coxswain for the Penn Athletic Club on the Schuylkill River and later became an all-city champion swimmer, specializing in the back stroke. When I was very young he had rave reviews in the sports section of the Philadelphia papers. One day, he won three races in three states: Pennsylvania, New Jersey, and Delaware. The first race was a mile or two down the Schuylkill River. The day before the race Dan and my father inspected the race course. Dan swam the course and found that the current was much stronger on the far bank than the close bank. When the starting gun sounded, he swam straight across the river while everyone else immediately swam downstream. Everyone thought him crazy until he reached the other side and easily passed the other swimmers, winning by a large margin. Immediately after that race, my father drove him over to Clementon Lake Park, outside Camden, New Jersey, where he won his second race of the day, and then on to Delaware for his triple crown.

Dan wanted to enter Yale, but at the age of sixteen it was decided that a year at a smaller local school would be better for him. At

Villanova College (now a university) he was asked to swim in an exhibition meet. He was promised that it would not really count as a competitive race. This was important because in those days if you competed for one college, you could never compete for another. When he applied for a swimming scholarship to Yale, it was denied because Villanova claimed that the meet in which he had participated was a regular competition meet. Many years later my cousin John Logue said to Dan that he thought it was a tragedy that Yale would not let him swim. Dan promptly replied, "Best thing that ever happened to me. I'd probably have become a high school swimming coach in South Jersey."

Even though we were broke at the time from the Crash of '29, Dan went on to Yale and succeeded as a scholar, athlete, and businessman. He sold ads for the *Yale Daily News,* brought in ten customers for a restaurant, and got free meals. He brought in more customers for suits at the best clothing store in New Haven and got free suits. He also became manager of the Yale Student Directory and made thousands of dollars, most of which he sent home. It was a tremendous help for the family.

I remember that Dan sent his laundry home each week and my mother would do it and send it back in a cardboard shipping box especially designed for students' laundry. The address label was in a little enclosure and could just be reversed for shipping back and forth. Finally, he worked a deal with a local laundry and had it done in New Haven free of charge.

I visited him at Yale one weekend when I was about eight. I met his roommate, Wesley Chin, a Chinese American from California. They kept their friendship for as long as my brother lived.

Dan posing with Jule on our front porch. 1926.

While I was staying with him in New Haven, Dan noticed a small bump over my eye. He took me to a doctor and the doctor extracted a bb that Leroy Schoch, a neighbor, had put there in a gun battle a few years before. No one, including myself or my mother, had ever noticed the bb and how close it had come to my eye.

I didn't see as much of him as I did my other siblings, but he was always good with me. If my sister Jule was my surrogate mother, Dan was my surrogate father, as he was always interested in me, not in a brotherly fashion—more in a fatherly one. That was OK by me. He was twice my age when he was just twenty and was worldly wise.

In the Navy ROTC, Dan sailed to Panama, San Juan, and Havana on a summer cruise. He drank at Sloppy Joe's Bar in Havana while on shore leave. The picture of him and his shipmates there has disappeared, but I remember seeing it many times.

After Yale he worked a short time for Carnegie Steel in Pittsburgh for the princely sum of $125 a month. He soon realized that was not for him and went to Yale Law School. After his first year at Yale Law School ended in May of 1941, the Navy called him up. He was given the command of a seventy-five-foot YP (Yard Patrol). The ship had belonged to Major Bowes of "The Major Bowes Original Amateur Hour," a radio show a bit similar to the recent and unlamented "Gong Show." His duty was to patrol the Delaware River in front of the Navy Yard to prevent saboteurs from doing any damage to our fighting ships then being built and tested there.

He once told me that had he gone to the University of Pennslyvania as he had first intended, he would have been in the 1939 Army ROTC. Most of that class of officers ended up in the Bataan Death March and few survived that torture. He would have been there had he not gone to Yale.

Being so young, I was allowed to visit him on his yacht. It had been commandeered by the Navy at the beginning of the national "Emergency." While the outside was painted battleship gray, the inside still had yellow and pink tiled bathrooms and a lavender blue galley.

I think Dan was always captain of his ship. Whenever he was promoted he got a bigger ship. By the end of the war he was one of the youngest lieutenant commanders in the Navy and commanded a large Assault Landing Ship, the USS *Doyan*. A ship that size was usually commanded by a full four-stripe captain. He took part in eight invasions in the South Pacific without a scratch. Once, while he was on the bridge overseeing the landing at Iwo Jima, an eight-inch

Japanese shell neatly pierced the crane boom about twenty feet in front of him. Had it not been a dud, that would have been the end of him.

I remember when Dan would come home each day from a summer job at the Atlantic Refinery in Philadelphia. He was about twenty-one and I was eleven. I would meet him at the end of our alley when he got off the bus and he would carry me home on his shoulders. I suppose it was just a few times but it seemed as if it was an everyday pleasure trip for me all summer long.

He helped everybody, our cousins, the Logues, through Yale, me at boarding school when our mother died, others in the family, and many hangers-on. He retired as CEO of Standex, a large conglomerate that he developed from his father-in-law's small plastics business. He had many friends and a few enemies. He originated a very profound comment about one particular person who had badmouthed him. "Why is he badmouthing me, I never helped him?" If you think about that adage, it does make practical sense.

Dan was following his wife home one afternoon in November of 1991 in Carmel, California. He had a massive heart attack and his car slowly drove into some hedges outside a firehouse. Within half a minute, the fire rescue paramedics were there. They were too late. He leaves three wonderful children and more than half a dozen grandchildren.

My Brother Dan at Iwo Jima.

Identified Flying Objects: Flying in the Thirties and Fifties

During the thirties there were all sorts of flying objects over our heads. The autogiro and the dirigible made major cameo appearances during that decade and many other kinds of gliders, monoplanes, and biplanes were also developed that held our adolescent interest.

♦ Gyroplanes ♦

Many people I speak to today have never heard of an autogiro and think I'm putting them on when I tell them how they used to land on the roof of the Main Post Office at 30th and Market streets in West Philadelphia, take on several air mail bags and whisk them to Central Airport in Camden, New Jersey, in just a few minutes. There, the bags would be quickly transferred to an Eastern Airlines DC-3 to be sent winging their way across the country, arriving at their destination in just two or three days.

While the autogiro, sometimes called a gyroplane, was invented in 1923 by Juan de la Cierva in Spain, it was greatly improved upon by Philadelphian Harold Pitcairn. The huge non-powered rotor on top of the plane spun and gave lift from the force of the regular propeller in the front of the plane. Rod and Wallace Kellett followed Pitcairn in further developing the autogiro. Both manufacturers produced ma-

An Eastern Airlines Kellet Autogyro taking off from the roof of the Main Post Office in Philadelphia in July, 1939, with a load of air mail bound for the old Philadelphia Airport in Camden, New Jersey.

chines with and without wings. Kellett's wingless version was adopted for a year's trial by the United States Post Office.

I used to stand outside the post office for hours waiting for the air mail plane to approach the four-story roof, head into the wind, and make a gentle landing. Within minutes, after unloading mail for Philadelphia, it would take on another load and be off for the five-minute flight to Central Airport. The whole operation must have saved ten or fifteen minutes over a fast mail truck but it was fun while the novelty lasted.

◆ Dirigibles ◆

As children we all discussed the merits of dirigibles as opposed to regular airplanes. I always favored the huge sky monsters because they could carry so many people in luxury. They could even take on a few small airplanes, much like an aircraft carrier.

To prove the practicability of lighter-than-air dirigibles, U.S. Navy Lieutenant Commander Charles E. Rosenthal, once boarded the *Akron* at Lakehurst, New Jersey. As the great ship flew down the Atlantic Coast, he climbed into one of five small fighter planes that were kept in a hangar *inside* the airship. Instead of a catapult launch, a big hook held the plane.

After his plane was lowered out of its belly, it was released from its hook and he flew it to Washington to an important meeting. Despite the promotion, when the *Akron* crashed some months later, the death knell of such craft was sounded.

The *Macon* was a sister ship of the *Akron* and crashed in the Pacific Ocean off Point Sur with two persons killed. Just last year, they discovered the wreck in 1,000 feet of water. The three or four fighter planes on board were still in place and apparently in excellent condition. There are plans to salvage the entire ship including the on-board pursuit planes.

I remember seeing a photograph of the sister ship to the *Akron,* the *Shenandoah,* standing on its nose during a storm. I don't know how the airship ever righted itself and continued on its journey. But it did.

My cousins had a first-day air mail cover of an air mail letter carried around the world by the *Graf Zeppelin.* When I visited them I always asked to see that special stamp.

Courtesy of Dayton University Archives

A US Navy Curtis F9C-2 Sparrowhawk hooking up to its mother airship, the Macon.

Many a summer night we sat on the back steps of Albert Orlando's house down the street and argued about which bomber or fighter plane was better. Soon after the Germans invaded Poland in 1939, Albert's older brother, who had a pilot's license, took a few of us to Mitchell Field, Long Island, where he signed up as a flying sergeant in the U.S. Army Air Corps. It was a thrill driving through the Holland and Midtown tunnels on our way to the air base. It was a greater thrill when we were given a tour of the base, which had small fabric-covered pursuit planes and a few huge Martin bombers. Today, one could most likely fit two of those old bombers into the maw of a C-17 Galaxy cargo plane. We weren't the first to have jumbo planes.

◆ The RAF ◆

During the Battle of Britain in the summer of 1940 the RAF sent a few Hurricane fighter planes over to the U.S. to promote solidarity and support for their cause. A group of us children traveled by suburban trolley to Wings Field near Norristown to watch a full day of dogfights, aerobatics, parachute jumps, and other daring escapades by the teenage heroes of the RAF. On that day I decided I would be a fighter pilot when it became my time to go to war. Alas, my astigmatism kept me on the ground.

◆ Popeye, the One-Eyed Pilot ◆

Now that half a century has passed and the statute of limitations has long since expired, I can relate the tale of my brother Ed's flying adventures. Ed lost his eye as a teenager to a stray snowball thrown over a fence. A few of his more irreverent friends called him Popeye after the one-eyed comic strip sailor.

Like me, Ed had a passion to fly and wasn't going to let having just one eye stop him. He went in for his medical exam and was told to hold a cardboard cover over one eye while he read the chart. First, he covered his glass eye and read the chart to the examiner's satisfaction. When asked to read with the other (his glass eye), he made a big shuffle of the card, changed hands, and again held the chart over his glass eye. He came through with flying (if you'll pardon the pun) colors and went on to spend many years safely flying in all sorts of planes. Once, perhaps after I wrecked his new car, he flew an open cockpit Stearman biplane to see his girlfriend in Washington. He recently told me that because of the impossible new regulations he doesn't pilot his own plane any more so I guess it's safe to tell this story.

◆ The Powered Glider of the Luftwaffe ◆

Shortly after the second war to end all wars, I found myself in Germany working in a motorcycle factory in Bad Hamburg, VdH (Von der Hohe—By the hill), which was run by the brother of my brother Dan's mother-in-law. One day I went to visit a friend of my host family in Wurzburg. Hans Wünscher was the inventor of an ingenious powered glider. He gave me photos of it. He developed it for the Luftwaffe when the Germans were forbidden an air force.

It was a smooth-looking craft and had a round tubular fuselage that connected the main body to the tail section. About three feet of the tube contained two-folded back propeller blades. After being towed to several thousand feet the glider would sail around, gradually losing altitude.

When the pilot felt he was too low he would pull a cord of the type on chain saws. The little motor would start up and the tube with the recessed, folded-back propellers would start to turn. The centrifugal force would force the props out and give the glider the power to rise up to a safer altitude. When that height was attained, the pilot would shut off the motor and the wind blast would force the two props back into their recessed tube.

I often wonder why the plane was never built and sold commercially. I'm sure this unique powered glider helped train many German fighter pilots at a time when it was forbidden by Allied sanctions.

◆ The 11th Airborne Division ◆

We left the reader at the tail end of World War II where I couldn't get into the Army Pilot Training Program because of an astigmatism. I didn't want to miss out on that war so I joined the Merchant Marine and visited twenty or thirty countries before I was twenty years old. If I was ever going to fly, I would have to wait for the next war to come along.

In my paranoia, I was convinced that my draft board in Andover, Massachusetts, waited for the Big War to end before they could send me my greetings. Less than a week after the North Koreans invaded South Korea in June of 1950, I received my induction notice to join the Army.

My best friend at the time, and until his death a few years ago, was Arthur (Archie) Keenan. A bona fide hero of World War II with four Purple Hearts, two Silver Stars, and other assorted medals, Archie had just a month before he obtained an ROTC commission as a second lieutenant. He too got his notice to report in a few weeks to the 101st Airborne Division at Camp Breckenridge, Kentucky. "Hey, Paul, when you get to the induction center, volunteer for Airborne and we'll be together and have a great war."

I took his advice and was soon on board a Pullman car prophetically named *Kismet* (Fate) bound for the 11th Airborne Division stationed at Fort Campbell, Kentucky. It turned out that the 101st at that time was not really airborne but just a lowly recruit training division living on past glories. But that's another story.

Apart from Archie's urging me to go Airborne, there was my not-so-latent desire to fly. If I couldn't pilot an airplane at least I could jump out of them. This is by the way of introducing a few humorous and not-so-humorous noncombat war stories.

◆ God Told Me Not To Jump ◆

One bright day in 1951 about two dozen of us boarded an old C-46 Curtiss Commando for a practice jump over the back woods of Kentucky. We were all prepared and standing up, having already checked our buddies' chutes. As the green light came on over the drop zone we started to push our way to the door. Suddenly the line stopped. Someone "froze in the door." It took our jumpmaster about ten seconds to push him out. By that time the red light came on signaling us not to jump, because in those ten seconds we had passed beyond the newly plowed dirt drop zone and were over a deeply wooded area. However, we were so caught up in the moment that we ignored the jumpmaster's order and flung ourselves out the door. We landed in tall trees and several of us had to cut ourselves out of our harnesses. I still carry my noncombat scar on my arm.

That night I asked the recalcitrant trooper why he froze in the door and caused the rest of his stick (line of paratroopers) such grief. We had to walk miles through the woods back to our transport. He said, "God told me not to jump." When I asked him why God waited until the last minute to talk to him and didn't tell him not to get in the plane before we took off, he had no answer. Our reluctant was "processed" out of the 11th before dawn the next day.

Meanwhile, we caught six kinds of hell from our company commander, Fred Metheny, first String All-American, Nebraska, 1941, and recipient of the Distinguished Service Cross, Bastogne, 1944. He told us that had we been on a combat jump and had gone out the door on a red light we would have landed in unprotected enemy territory and would have all been killed. That lesson of not being a robot has stayed with me all my life.

◆ I Think Not, Corporal ◆

Among other jobs I had in the Airborne was that of regimental photographer. During Arctic maneuvers at Fort Drum, New York, in the winter of 1952, Secretary of the Army Frank Pace came to visit.

We had a wonderful California bobcat as a mascot and were always proud to show him off to VIPs. As Secretary Pace came near Squeaky, our beautiful and fierce-looking mascot, I suggested, "Mr. Secretary,

I would really appreciate a photograph of you petting our mascot." It was very brave of me to make this request because there were all sorts of two-, three-, and four-star generals present. Secretary Pace smiled, and said, "I'm sure you would, Corporal, but I think not."

A dozen years later I met Mr. Pace at a Washington cocktail party and reminded him of the incident. He said, "I remember the incident well, and I still think I made the right choice not to pet your mascot."

◆ How to Get to New York on a Three-Day Pass ◆

I guess the greatest trick I pulled while in the Army was chartering a DC-3. It was the Labor Day weekend in 1951. I had a hot date in New York and when I arrived at the Nashville Airport I found that there wasn't a single seat available to New York for three days. As we never knew when we would be released from duty we couldn't make our reservations in advance.

There was a crowd of GIs milling about the airport, bemoaning their plight. I called an air charter service on the other side of the field and asked the man in charge if he had a DC-3 available. He said sure and I asked if he'd give me a free ride if I filled his plane with New York–bound passengers. He readily agreed to the bargain.

I stood on a table in the Nashville Airport and announced that I was chartering a DC-3 that would be leaving for New York in a half hour. Immediately a line formed and I took the names of twenty-six GIs, from lowly privates to exalted majors. I must say, it was a good feeling for me, a mere corporal, to have a major standing in my line.

I called the owner of the DC-3 and told him I had a planeload ready to go. In ten minutes he taxied over, set up a small table, and took the regular air fares from the twenty-six men. Within minutes we were airborne on our way to New York and I got a free ride!

◆ The Airborne Rite of Passage ◆

The development of our aircraft from 1950 to 1952 was truly astonishing. We began the decade with slow-moving, low altitude, non-pressurized C-46s (Curtiss Commandos) and C-47s (Dakotas). As the doors wouldn't open in flight we flew with no doors with the minus-40-degree weather blasting through our plane. Later we got C-82s and then C-119 Flying Box Cars. They were a luxury as we could keep warm until they opened the doors just prior to a jump. By the time my tour was over in 1952 we were jumping out of giant C-124

Globemasters. The double-decked Globemasters held about 240 troops, ten times what the old World War relics carried! But I still preferred the old proven warhorses with no doors.

Anyway, the old planes had very primitive toilet facilities. On long hauls of four or five hours, we had to use a relief tube much like a hospital bed urinal. It was a hose attached to the side of the plane in the rear.

A new trooper would usually ask a veteran what the purpose of the tube was and we would all immediately take on a role. "Why, that's the speaking tube the jumpmaster uses to talk to the pilot in case the intercom breaks down." "Oh yeah?" said the dupe. "Yeah," we said, "you just pick up the tube, put it to your mouth, and talk to the captain." "What do I say," said the novice. "Oh, anything—like, 'this is Private Jones, can you tell me our air speed, altitude, and ETA.'"

"Really?" said the mark. He would then go over to the "speaking tube," pick it up, and ask the pilot the questions we suggested. Then he would put the tube to his ear to listen for a response. When none was forthcoming we advised him to hold the tube closer to his mouth and shout louder. He did this a few times and we would tell him that the pilot was probably too busy to entertain the troops with idle chatter. The recruit would finally give up and return to his seat. Then one or two of us would get up and go to the hose urinal and relieve ourselves. The now more experienced soldier would be flabbergasted and turn from red to purple while the rest of us shook the plane with laughter. Another rite of passage had been celebrated.

One more noncombat war story. As I&E NCO of the 511th AIR (Information and Education Non-Commissioned Officer for the 511th Airborne Infantry Regiment), I was sent to the Armed Forces Information School at Fort Slocum, New York. Fort Slocum was a small island off New Rochelle in Long Island Sound, and better duty one could not hope for. The course lasted six weeks, and three or four nights a week and every weekend were spent in the Big Apple. We had to study hard but it was worth it. A few days before graduation someone came to take a group photo of our class, which was made up of both men and women from all branches of the Armed Forces.

The photographer had one of those old-fashioned panoramic cameras that swiveled on a tripod. We all assembled in a semi-circle in front of the camera and were told to stay very still as the camera panned across us from right to left.

Me and our California bobcat mascot, Squeaky.

I positioned myself at the very far right end of the hundred or so service people. As soon as the camera passed me, I ran around the back and stood very still at the left end of the group a scant few seconds before the slow-panning camera reached me. Thus I appeared twice in the same photograph!

Shortly before we were to head back to our respective posts the commanding officer of the base called me in. As I saluted in my report to him I noticed the group photo spread out on his desk. He said nothing and I said nothing. He looked at me and then at the photograph and then back to me. I'm sure I detected the slightest of smiles as he said, "That will be all, Corporal."

I've searched for that photograph for years and years. Next to the one of me with my arms around our California bobcat mascot, that group photo was my favorite from the Airborne.

When the next war (Vietnam) came along, I joined the Peace Corps and went to Colombia.

Now I read in my Airborne newsletter that the Russian, Thai, Honduran, Brazilian, and who knows what air forces are offering jump wings to paratroop veterans of any age who visit their country, undergo a one- or two-day refresher course and make two jumps from their planes and, incidentally, pay a hefty fee. I'm sorely tempted!

While I got out a full corporal, my friend Archie stayed in the Army and retired a full bird colonel. We remained friends for forty years. He died a few years ago and on my last visit to him at the Milwaukee Veterans Hospital he asked me to take care of his wife. Kathy has been with me three years now and we are in for the long haul.

Ed with our nephew Denny and niece Barrie Hogan. 1946.

Ed catching up with the news in the fifties.

My Brother Ed

Leprosy,
My God you've got leprosy
Was that your eyeball
That fell into my highball?

My brother Ed was struck in the eye by an ice-laden snowball thrown over a fence as he passed by a school yard at the age of fourteen. We never found out who threw the snowball and I doubt if the thrower ever knew of the terrible consequences of his action.

I was just eight at the time but I remember vividly the pain and suffering Ed experienced for months before they decided that they couldn't save his eye and had to remove it. He entered Wills Eye Hospital in Philadelphia and came home a few days later with just one eye.

Ed certainly made the best of a bad situation and, except for being classified 4F during the war, did just about everything anyone with two eyes did. As I have already related, he even got a pilot's license!

Spike Jones's Leprosy Song could have been about my brother Ed. To shock or titillate a girlfriend, he would sometimes remove the olive from her martini and slip in a spare glass eye. You can imagine the reaction of a young woman, ready to sip her drink and seeing an eyeball in the bottom of her glass. He had several glass eyes always ready as spares. The same one would sometimes irritate his eye socket after several days and he would have to change. One eye had a martini glass instead of a pupil and another had a naked lady where the pupil should be. Sometimes, while on a date, he would appear with his naked lady glass eye. His date would not be aware of the change until they were sitting at a table and looking into each other's eyes. The date would react in unexpected ways.

One story about Ed I forgot to include in the Cape May chapter was about his nearly electrocuting my Aunt Rene. One summer, he arrived at the Logues' summer home with two big suitcases. When my aunt opened them she found not a stitch of clothing, but a mass of electric gear, wires, transformers, radios, an inter-office communications system, and a myriad of gadgets, tools, and whatnot. Ed had to borrow clothes from his siblings and cousins.

At Cape May he tried to emulate Benjamin Franklin's famous kite experiment. He climbed onto the roof of the three-story summer house and threaded wire down the side and into the Logue boys' bedroom window. From there, the wire ran along the floor to some sort of transformer. During a severe thunderstorm, lightning struck the cable he had rigged up while my Aunt Rene was in the room. It knocked her down and dazed her. After she had gathered herself together, she let her displeasure with Ed's experiment be known, and the wires were immediately taken down.

At home, too, Ed always had gadgets around to make things easier. When my mother was bedridden, he hooked up a three- or four-station intercom so that she could communicate with us while in bed. When Ed was a young teenager, I remember him in our basement workshop making jigsaw puzzles. He would paste pictures onto thin plywood and cut intricate sections with his jigsaw. I know he sold some, but I don't think he made a living from that endeavor.

While a sixteen-year-old student at Overbrook High School Ed worked part time for a garage that specialized in repairing gangsters' cars. More than once he drove home in a bullet-riddled car borrowed from his boss. He finally saved up enough money to buy a 1936 Ford convertible with a two-speed rear. After getting up to seventy or eighty miles an hour, he would push or pull a lever which would activate the high-speed rear and increase his speed and efficiency by twenty or thirty percent. I loved to ride around with him in that car. It was sky blue and had a wide diagonal red stripe on each door.

Ed was and still is the daredevil and experimenter of the family. He has delved into everything, from diving helmets in the thirties to a means of creating power sources out of water in the seventies and, recently, to increasing the number of wave bands on FM radio by some strange method.

Since he had but one eye, he was ineligible for the draft. As soon as things started to heat up in 1940, he went to Puerto Rico and helped on the construction of Borinquen Field, the biggest air base ever constructed up to that time. He helped bring our brother John down to drive a bulldozer.

After the stint in Puerto Rico he worked for Matthew McCloskey, a big Philadelphia contractor who had a contract with the government to build concrete ships in Tampa. One day, during a lunch break, Ed, a very experienced bulldozer operator, decided he'd try to run a big new crane that McCloskey managed to get despite the acute shortage of such equipment at that time. He climbed in and spun the crane around so fast that the giant machine turned over on its side, sustaining much cosmetic damage.

From then on, whenever Matt McCloskey came to inspect the shipyard, there was one specially qualified crane operator whose sole job was to keep turning the bashed-in side of the crane away from Mr. McCloskey. Wherever McCloskey went, the crane would turn so that he would never see the damage and go berserk. President Kennedy appointed Matt ambassador to Ireland, a post now held by President Kennedy's sister.

Ed's two best friends, Jim Lynch and Phil Kellaher, traveled with him around the Caribbean on all those exotic construction jobs. To prove their friendship, whenever Ed had a date with a local lovely, they would steal his glass eye while he was taking a shower. He'd have to go on his date with a makeshift patch. Finally, he got a spare eye and took it into the shower with him.

After Pearl Harbor, Ed went with the Army Corps of Engineers to Trinidad, to build more air bases for the crucial air route to North Africa. Then on to Surinam, where he drove a bulldozer, panned for gold, and shot a jaguar (before there was such a thing as an endangered species). He sent me a gold nugget that he had panned on the Orinoco and gave me a gold *fica* (fist in Portuguese) good luck charm. I lost both souvenirs but still know how to make a Brazilian *fica* to wish someone good luck.

As the chain of airfields through Colombia, Venezuela, the three Guineas and on to Natal, Brazil, developed, Ed followed along until we had a South Atlantic air route to supply our forces in North Africa. In those days planes did not have the range to fly the North Atlantic. Besides, the German Navy and its U-boats had the North Atlantic pretty much under their control.

Ed came home in June of 1944 and began working for my brother Dan's father-in-law in Lawrence, Massachusetts. I had just finished my junior year at Lower Merion High School and was living with my Aunt Rene. Ed wrote me a letter suggesting that I could move in with him in his new apartment in nearby Andover when school started in September.

As the common expression goes, "I was outta there." In three days, I packed everything I could, hitchhiked to Andover, and moved in on him. We made a great "odd couple" until April of 1945 when I got an early diploma from Andover High and at seventeen joined the Merchant Marine.

Ed and Cynthia now live in Carmel, California, and we see each other three or four times a year. He still tries to steal ice cream from me by distracting me, saying, "Boy, look at that beautiful babe." I still humor him by turning my head.

While constructing air fields in Surinam, South America in 1942, Ed took time off to track down a marauding jaguar that was stalking the camp. A half century later, he'd go to jail for such activities.

The Hamilton and the Overbrook

While the first movie I ever saw was *The Phantom of the Opera* in my brothers' basement theater, the first real movie theater I ever went to was the Overbrook Theater at 63rd and Haverford Avenue, a ten-block walk from our house. I was six.

The main feature was *Roman Scandals* starring Eddie Cantor. I recall seeing everyone wearing togas and riding in chariots while Eddie

Eddie Cantor in Roman Scandals, the first movie I saw in a real theater. 1933.

Cantor, with his bulging eyes, was running from or chasing Roman soldiers.

Right next to the OB (our acronym for the Overbrook Theater) was Gus's Hoagie Shop. I'm sure this Italian sandwich, known in some areas as the heroe or submarine, was invented by Gus. Hoagies were sold in ten-, fifteen-, or twenty-five-cent sizes. I couldn't eat even a ten-cent Hoagie let alone a twenty-five-cent version. I would always split it with someone.

To get good seats at ten cents we always arrived at the OB about an hour ahead of show time. One of us would stand in line to get the best seats and the other would buy a ten-cent Hoagie. Hoagie was my nickname all through my adolescence! We would nibble at our sandwiches while in line but would save the biggest part to enjoy during the show. They were loaded with all sorts of cold cuts, exotic cheeses, hot peppers, garlic, tomatoes, lettuce and best of all, lots of onions. As hundreds of kids had terrible onion breath like ourselves, it never bothered us.

What I remember most was the incredible number of kids at the theater. Not only was every seat taken but there were two lines of kids sitting on the floor on each side of the two main aisles. The fire code must have been violated by an extra three or four hundred kids!

The Overbrook was a pretty fancy neighborhood theater; it cost just a dime until the City of Philadelphia decided to put a 10-percent tax on amusements and the ticket price soared to eleven cents. It eventually became a bakery and I never could even buy a roll there, preferring to remember its wonderful life as a neighborhood movie palace.

Our other theater of choice, only five blocks from my house, was the Hamilton. The Ham wasn't as classy as the OB but since it was closer we favored it. The program started at 1 P.M. with a Pathè newsreel. That weekly news program ignited my lifelong interest in current events.

Next on the program was a cartoon—Felix the Cat or Mickey Mouse and Donald Duck. After the cartoon there was some sort of popular science film. One of these films showed how quickly a home could be transformed to accommodate unexpected guests. To change the decor, the wife just pulled down a completely new wallpaper that was on window shades. Since the room wasn't quite large enough, the husband pushed a button and the whole wall moved out to double the interior space. As for changing sheets, the wife merely turned a crank at the bottom of the bed. The bottom sheet must have been a half-mile long on rollers at the foot and head of the bed. Merely by turning the crank a few turns a fresh part of the sheet replaced the dirty one.

For fifty years I wondered why anyone would go to the trouble of making a wall go in and out. Why not just leave it out? I wondered how you could wash a sheet that was five feet wide and a half-mile long. Half a century later, I finally figured the whole movie short was just a joke that I hadn't understood.

After the pop sci film came the serial where Dick Tracy faced certain death each week at the hands of Pruneface or Flattop. Then Flash Gordon would go through thirteen weeks of a desperate struggle with Ming The Merciless, and ended each chapter with Flash at Merciless' mercy. All week long we would discuss Dick and Flash's fate and offer opinions as to how they could escape from such hopeless situations. We all knew they would survive because the death of either one would end the series, but we could rarely figure out how they could manage it.

One of the Dick Tracy serials featured a beautiful flying wing plane much like the B-48 designed and flown by Northorp a decade later. Another hero had a biplane that could be picked up and reprovisioned by a Navy dirigible. For a few years in the mid-thirties the U.S. Navy really did have fighter plane pick-up capability.

Just before the main feature, usually a cowboy movie, came the Great Race. On paying our eleven-cent admissions we were each given a ticket numbered 1 to 10. We held on to these tickets for the Great Race. Each week the Ham would show a crazy race. Each race had ten entrants, and every participant had a large number on his front and back. One week they would race in crazy boats made of everything from old bathtubs to inner tubes holding up a sofa. The racers would paddle the sofa or bathtub down a river race course, swamping whomever they could, pulling the plug on the bathtub, setting fire to the sofa, doing whatever they could do to win the race.

The next week there would be road races in which ten men on bicycles, or hospital beds with big wheels, or the same sofa with wheels would race down a country road. The road would have as many obstacles as the river course. Several hundred kids, the entire audience, would stand and shout for their number to win.

No one could be sure that his man would win because at the last second a lagging number would come up from behind and win the race. When the turtle beat the hare, ten percent of the kids who had a matching winning number would line up. They mounted the stage to receive their candy bar reward trophy from the manager. The other ninety percent of the audience would boo the manager, the theater and the winners. The winners would savor both the win and the candy bar out of all proportion to the monetary value. The featured western film would be almost anticlimactic after the Great Race.

The other week on the evening news I saw that two police officers were shot in a gun battle with drug pushers just outside what was the Hamilton Theater. The bakery that occupied the Overbrook Theater is boarded up. I'm going to try to find a video of *Roman Scandals* to see if it still impresses me as it did then, sixty years ago.

The Hamilton Theater today.

The Faint Check

The Studio movie theater at 16th & Market streets in Philadelphia had an interesting life before it fell under the wrecker's ball in the name of urban renewal. In the beginning it was a typical movie house. Then it became a house of horror films and finally a single X-rated theater. That was before XXX-rated theaters were allowed.

We frequented the Studio during the double horror show phase of its life. About once a month our gang of about ten twelve-year-olds would hop on the rear of the Number 41 trolley and hang on for the twenty-block ride to the Market Street Elevated station at 63rd Street. There we would "shoot" (our personal slang for "pick up") transfers dropped by considerate riders. I don't think they were litterbugs, as the free transfers were the only thing dropped on the ground around the station. We turned in the transfers and got a free ride into the city.

We usually headed for the Studio Theater where there was always a double horror show, each more bloody than the previous week. As a special come-on the theater would give all the customers Faint Checks which could be redeemed for a return visit in case the patron fainted in reaction to the horrible scenes.

Once there, we would each chip in a penny so that one of us could purchase a ticket and open up a rear fire exit door for the rest of us to pile in. We would rush in, scatter and sit down as though we were paying customers. We'd sit through a double feature and then leave quietly—filled with the terror of the gruesome films.

For one of us—not me of course—a free movie was not enough. My pal would find a discarded Faint Check in the aisle. He would wait for a particular bloodthirsty scene, scream, and "faint," falling in the middle of the aisle. The ushers were on to us and usually ignored us. By the time my pal demanded a return ticket after having "fainted," we were out the door. The management threatened him with all sorts of charges from unlawful entry to fraud and embezzlement. After two or three failed attempts at this particular type of extortion, my pal finally gave up and was satisfied with a free movie and no fringe benefits.

After the movie we repaired to the nearest Horn & Hardart Automat where we would eat the food left on the plates before the waitresses had a chance to clean the tables.

Fully sated spiritually and gastronomically, we returned to the 15th Street station, "shooted" more free transfers, and rode the subway/elevated train back to 63rd Street. As there were always lots of transfers lying around we didn't have to hop on the back of the 41 trolley but rode home in style, just like paying passengers.

Making Money

In the depths of the Depression, no one had the means to purchase a home, and so my father, a house builder, had no work. As is being done in many industries today, my father had to drastically downsize his business. To compensate we invented various family money-making enterprises.

One minuscule business was making Japanese gardens for sale to friends and neighbors. At a sale, my father bought very large glass fish bowls about eighteen inches in diameter. Into each bowl he'd put about four inches of good topsoil. Then he'd add two or three interestingly shaped rocks which in miniature appeared to be gigantic boulders. He would then add a blanket of moss to cover the dirt, and create little paths made from tiny white pebbles.

I loved to help him gather moss. Not content with obtaining it close to home, he used to drive out to Gulph Mills on the road to Valley Forge. We stopped near historic Hanging Rock by a small, fast-running stream. The rock hung far out over the road. It still hangs over the road today, sixty years later, but far less than it used to, having been hit by over a thousand trucks in the intervening years. I drive under the rock every month or so and have instant recall of my childhood forays with my father.

After the expeditions, we'd drive home with several boxes of deep green plush moss for the gardens. To add still more realism, my father would put tiny ceramic highly arched Japanese bridges over narrow

Historic Hanging Rock in Gulph Mills, PA.

streams made from small gray pebbles. In the more elaborate gardens, he would place small kimono-clad geishas with tiny parasols.

In his top-of-the-line gardens he would place a wee four-story pagoda on the top of a hill no more than an inch or two high. Somewhere, my father got very tiny tree-like plants to add even more realism to the scene. That was long before anyone ever heard of century-old Bonsai trees.

After the garden was complete, he would add just a bit of water and place a round glass lid over the top of the bowl. The lid would not only seal in the moisture but would help to create moisture by condensation, so one rarely needed to water the garden.

I don't know how many he sold or how much they cost. We seemed to have quite a few around the house at the time so I guess our friends and neighbors didn't have much money to buy these lovely little gardens. Now there are books about the subject but we were the first in our neighborhood to have a Japanese garden.

For a year or so when I was about ten years old, I sold and delivered *The Saturday Evening Post*. A man would drop a big bundle at our house every Friday. They sold for a nickel and I made about one and a half cents on each. Curtis Publishing once ran a promotion scheme and I somehow made more money by buying a certain amount of *Posts* and just giving them away to friends. I forgot how my scam worked, but I made over a quarter a week at it until the promotion campaign ended.

Another project that didn't make us millionaires was making and selling planters from used coffee cans and clothespins. I think that was a project of my brothers Dan and Ed, but I'm not sure. My brothers would have the neighbors save their old coffee cans for pick up. They would paint a dozen or so at a time and set them out to dry. Then they would paint old-fashioned, two-pronged clothespins a bright color. On the really fancy flower pots, they would dip the round heads of the clothespins into a brightly contrasting color paint. After everything dried, they would mount the pins around the edge of the coffee cans, fill the cans with dirt, stick a plant in them, and try to sell them up and down the street.

They also sold decorated cans without plants. I think they asked a quarter for the empty cans and half a dollar for those with plants in them. They sold quite a few pots, but I suspect it was because the clothespins on the cans were WORTH more than the finished product and our neighbors knew a bargain when they saw one.

That enterprise didn't last too long. Besides my mother needed the pins to hang up the wash.

Model Mack Trucks like those my brother Ed found submerged in the flooded quarry.

Great Inventions of the Thirties

During the thirties our home at 6044 Columbia Avenue was Menlo Park, Silicon Valley, and Akademgorodok (Academic City), Russia, all rolled in one. My oldest brother, Dan was the neighborhood Milton Friedman. Everything he touched turned into money and he rarely, if ever, got his hands dirty.

My other two brothers resembled the comic strip characters Calvin and Hobbes and their real-life counterparts, one a theologian, the other, a philosopher. Ed was (and still is) the flamboyant and adventuresome Calvin. John was the scholar, the brilliantly contemplative and stoic Hobbes.

Ed once found an abandoned Harley-Davidson motorcycle in a nearby quarry. It had no tires, brakes, lights, or even a seat. He pushed it to the top of the 61st Street hill by our house, climbed on board, and rocketed down the hill, careening onto Lancaster Avenue, also known as U.S. Route 30, the Lincoln Highway. He didn't hit anyone, and no one hit him.

Another time, Ed put wings on the front of his bike and tore down that 61st Street hill. He had neglected to install a tail stabilizer. When he got up speed, the front of his bike became airborne while the rear stayed grounded. He flipped over backwards but fortunately landed on his head and wasn't injured.

♦   Ed's Diving Helmet   ♦

Until I found a 1934 copy of *Mechanix Illustrated* last year, I always thought my brother Ed had invented the five- gallon-can diving helmet.

Back in 1934, he decided to build a diving helmet to explore a local quarry that had flooded several years before.

He got a five-gallon paint can, cleaned it out, cut out a circle in the side for a window, tinsnipped two cuts in the edge so the helmet would fit over his shoulders, and drilled a small hole in the bottom (now the top) for an air hose. He found a round piece of safety glass and secured it to the hole in a manner that would be waterproof. He padded the sharp edges of the shoulder cuts so the helmet would fit snugly and smoothly over his shoulders. Next, he attached about a hundred feet of rubber hose from the top of his helmet to a bicycle pump.

We all drove out to the quarry for the first test dive. He donned the helmet, attached about twenty-five pounds of scrap iron to his belt, and walked down the quarry road into the water. Meanwhile a team of pumpers manned the flimsy bicycle pump to force air into his helmet.

As he disappeared down the submerged road, bubbles marked his trail. After a few minutes—it seemed like hours—he walked back up the road clutching a Mack Bulldog radiator ornament that he had managed to wrench off one of the sunken dump trucks abandoned during the great flood.

When I came across the old "how to" magazine last year, I sent it to Ed with a note saying, "Now I know where you got the idea." He confessed that that was where he got his brainstorm, and has since renewed his subscription to *Popular Mechanics*.

♦   John's Surf Board   ♦

As I have said, my brother John was more like the comic strip character Hobbes. While his inventions were less dramatic and world-shaking, they were usually, but not always, more practical. For instance, he invented (unless, like Ed, he saw it in an undiscovered copy of *Popular Mechanics*) a cellular surfboard. This was decades before the development of the foam-filled Fiberglass surfboards that seem to adorn the roof of every Volkswagen Beetle in California.

He found an old wood ironing board. (They really were made of wood in those days.) Then he scavenged a couple of dozen metal beer cans. The beer cans were made of tin-plated steel and had to be opened with a triangular "church key." They were very strong. He cut some of the cans into tiny pieces and soldered the triangular openings closed. After the cans were all sealed he tested them for leaks in my mother's washtub. He then mounted them on either side of the bottom of the ironing board by drilling four holes in the board for each can. Finally, he then wired them tight to form a line along each bottom edge.

The initial testing in our flooded garage pool went off without a hitch. His surfboard had perfect buoyancy. His eighty-five-pound weight hardly caused a ripple as he paddled around the garage. But the real test would come in the Atlantic Ocean at Cape May when we went there to visit our cousins, the Logues.

At Cape May we water warriors geared up for the battle. Under combat conditions, unfortunately, the surf board didn't perform to expectations. It was fine when John simply paddled around in still water, but the first time he caught a big wave that drove him to shore, half the cans ripped off when he hit bottom. I don't remember if he went back to the drawing board or just went on to the next invention.

◆ Italy, 1943 ◆

John was also inventive under real combat conditions. Before the war ended, John would have seen nearly 1,000 days of hard combat with a Combat Engineers Battalion in Africa, Sicily and Italy. John drove a big D-8 Caterpillar bulldozer doing everything from clearing roads for the advancing infantry by pushing burned-out tanks and trucks off the road to helping build the first Bailey Bridge across the Arno River in Florence, thereby helping save the historic, centuries-old Ponte Vecchio.

Each night, he would remove the distributor and take it into his sleeping bag to prevent anyone from stealing his baby. He awoke to find his bulldozer gone. His company commander was furious and was ready to have a statement of charges made against John for the cost of the monster. On a corporal's pay, it would have taken him about 20 years to pay back Uncle Sam for losing his bulldozer.

John asked for and got a three-day pass to look for his machine. A few hours short of his seventy-two-hour grace period, he was seen trundling up to the battalion command post in what was presumed his bulldozer.

Somehow it looked newer and cleaner than the stolen one. But it had the same serial number painted on each side of the hood, even though the numbers seemed freshly painted. John's company commander came out and, with an almost imperceptible grin, looked up at my brother and said "I don't want to hear about it, sergeant."

From then until John helped to liberate Milan and saw Mussolini and his mistress hanging upside down, John's bulldozer was rarely out of sight. He slept either on or near it for over a year, and he piled empty Jerry gas cans on it to sound an alarm if it started to sleep-crawl in the middle of the night. He told me that next to his day of discharge, the happiest day of his Army career was when he signed off on his bulldozer and gave it back to Uncle Sam.

John aboard his "liberated" bulldozer, Italy. 1944.

Nurse Chinfanny

I was involved in a tricycle accident when I was just three years old. I somehow suffered a hernia when I collided with a playmate on his trike. I had to wait until I reached puberty before I could be operated on. When my hernia swelled up my father would hang me by my heels until the swelling receded. When I grew too heavy for him, I learned to either stand on my head or push the swelling back with my hand. I wasn't too happy with that benign but bothersome malady.

When I reached adolescence my mother took me to the Thomas Jefferson Hospital in downtown Philadelphia for a consultation. We were fortunate to have Mr. and Mrs. Prickett as close neighbors. Mrs. Prickett, who had a cat named Putter, somehow connected to the administration at Jefferson Memorial Hospital, and through her my mother had me admitted at a very nominal charge.

After school vacation began in the summer of 1940, I was admitted to "Jeff" and spent a day or two in bed getting prepped for surgery. It was very embarrassing when a nurse shaved me just prior to going into the operating theater. I felt panic when the nurse clasped a mask over my face while breathing in the foul-tasting ether.

The next thing I knew was that I awoke to the smiling face of my nurse, Miss Chinfanny. Her cool hand soothed my fevered brow and she allowed me a small sip of luke warm water. I was starving and nauseous, thirsty and hurting all at once but except for the few drops of water and Nurse Chinfanny's smile, I got nothing for 24 hours.

The next day and for a few days after I was given a very thin broth with a few crackers. I had to remain quite still and wasn't allowed to turn over for fear that the sutures would come apart. Finally I was permitted to sit up and given more substantial nourishment. I was placed in a ward with about twenty men. I was the only child. My fellow adult patients were very interesting and I heard World War I being fought all over again with the Army vets trying to outwar the Navy vets and vice versa. I heard about the terrible battles fought in France and the dangers of sub chasing on the North Atlantic in winter.

The men treated me as one of their own. I never felt that they looked down on me, nor did they make fun of my youth and inexperience. They regaled me with many exciting adventures and they enjoyed each other's company with jokes and lies and general bantering back and forth.

I soon fell hopelessly in love with Nurse Chinfanny and resorted to all sorts of tricks to attract her attention. I had brought with me a small toy. It was a Tootsie Toy model of a Buck Rogers' rocket ship. The space ship was about four inches long and had spherical command modules at each end. There was a small pulley on the top of each sphere through which one could insert a string. By tying one end of the string to a post or having another boy hold it one could make the rocket ship go back and forth on the string. Making the string steep made the rocket ship go faster. The toy gave me many hours of diversion. We had no radio to listen to, let alone a TV to watch during our convalescence.

One time, when I especially wanted to make a flirtatious contact with Nurse Chinfanny, I waited until she walked down the aisle on her rounds. I had already thrown the weighted rocket ship string over the curtain rod of the patient opposite me. As my heart-throb walked down the aisle I lowered the string until it snagged her cap and threw it to the floor. All the men were watching this event but none gave me away. When she retrieved her hat she discovered the string and my trick. All the men laughed and she smiled, but admonished me to be good. Although she feigned disapproval, I know she was secretly pleased with the attention I showered on her. At least I think she was pleased.

I was in the hospital a total of twenty days! After two weeks I was allowed to get out of bed and sit in a wheel chair. I tore from one ward to another in my new-found freedom.

A historic aviation event occurred that summer and I had a grand stand seat on the tenth-floor balcony. The newspapers told of a large flight of new B-17 bombers which would pass over downtown Philadelphia on their way from Kelly Field in Texas to Mitchell Field on Long Island. Those of us who could crowded the balcony until we heard a loud droning from the southwest sky. It was the most thrilling show, except when the gigantic dirigible *Hindenberg* flew right over my house at just a few hundred feet four years before. It wasn't until this year that I finally got inside a real B-17-G at the Planes of Fame Air Museum at the Flying Cloud Airport near Minneapolis. At that time I also took my first trip in an open air Stearman PT-17 Navy Trainer, a relic from World War II.

On the twentieth day of my sentence, I was allowed to go home. Miss Chinfanny wheeled me to the exit where my mother waited. My heroine told my mother what a good patient I was, never referring to my antics with the space ship. As she helped me into our car Nurse Chinfanny gave me a kiss! I was totally smitten and spoke hardly a word on the way home.

Forty years later I suffered another hernia. I had a brief consultation with Dr. Parker who specialized in what is called the Canadian Procedure. He had performed the operation several thousand times and I completely trusted him. I entered Phoenixville Hospital late one

The rocket ship I used to snag Nurse Chinfanny's cap. 1940.

night, went to bed, and was rousted out at 6 the next morning. I had to walk to the operating theater and my surgeon ordered me to climb onto the operating table. I was given a local and the doctor, nurses, and anesthesiologist all joked as they went to work.

After the surgeon sewed up my inner skin layer he ordered me to do three sit ups while a nurse held my feet. I couldn't believe what he said, harking back forty years to my first hernia operation. I did the three situps and then he ordered me to strain as hard as I could to burst the stitches. Again I complied and, satisfied, the surgeon sewed up my outer skin. "Better to break the stitches now than later," he said.

As soon as he was done and the nurses placed a bandage on the cut, he ordered me to get off the table and walk back to my room with the admonition that I should walk forty-five minutes every hour until 10 P.M. Leaning on a nurse, I staggered back to my room, only to be denied my bed as I had to walk for the required three-quarters of an hour. The doctor came by my room at 9 P.M. and caught me in bed, gave me a bawling out, and ordered the nurses to keep me out of bed until 10 P.M. He asked me what I would be doing at home had I not had the operation that day. I told him I'd be chopping wood for the next winter. "OK," he said, "Chop for four hours tomorrow and six hours the next day and whatever you do, don't be taking naps and such."

So much for modern medicine. I didn't even have Miss Chinfanny to nurse me. It's a cruel world.

The Organ Grinder

One of our favorite street vendors in the thirties was the Monkey Man. He carried a hand-cranked organ that played as many as ten different tunes. His monkey was a little guy dressed up like a soldier or a clown or perhaps a doorman.

From late spring through early fall, the Monkey Man would come down our alley about once a month. During school times he would come in the late afternoon because he always got a penny from children but rarely anything from adults.

We would hear him the minute he entered our alley with his music machine strapped over his shoulder. When a few of us gathered around he would set down his one-legged organ and crank out beautiful tunes. We begged pennies from our parents to put in the little fellow's hand.

The monkey, whose name I think was Georgie, would climb into our arms. We would then place a penny into his tiny fingers. He would then jump down, tip his hat to us, run over to his master, fork over his penny, and come back to us for more pennies.

There were several other organ grinders who visited our alley. One had a wooden leg that matched the wooden leg of his organ. Another had what seemed like a piano to us. It was a large box about three feet wide and sat on wheels. He pushed rather than carried it and his monkey rode on top until it was show time, when the monkey would then go into his routine of begging, grabbing pennies and tipping his hat.

We never saw the organ grinders or their monkeys in the winter-time. Later I learned that all the organ grinders went south to Florida or Louisiana because their pets couldn't stand the cold Philadelphia winters.

In those days I never thought about the economics of organ grinders, but later I read that an already-trained monkey would sell for around $100 and an organ for as much as $300. Multiply that by about twenty times to account for inflation and you have a pretty expensive investment. Organ grinders earned about $20 to $25 a week. That isn't very much for a self-employed business man—the equivalent of about $400 today.

You can still see organ grinders with little monkeys, but they seem to be young college types on a lark. The old-time organ grinders raised their entire families on the pennies we gave for a bit of entertainment in our alley.

Jule in our back yard playing with the organ grinder's monkey. 1927.

My P-40 Skato

I think the skatos we built ourselves in the thirties were more fun than today's skateboards. Perhaps that's because I haven't really mastered the updated version of what we used to play on. I mean who cares to do flips up the sides of an empty swimming pool wall or stand on one's hands going down a steep hill in the middle of traffic?

Our skatos were simple and cost next to nothing. There were three basic parts: an old pair of steel-wheeled skates, a two-by-four board about 4 feet long, and a sturdy orange crate. As the war clouds were forming over China we romanticized the Flying Tigers and gave fighter plane names to our machines. Mine was a Curtis P-40 fighter, complete with two machine guns! Roller skates in those days had heavy steel wheels with ball bearings and could be adjusted to fit any size shoe. They didn't have four single

Michael Keenan on his crateless skato.

Skato race in New York in the thirties.

plastic wheels in a row and didn't take the fifteen minutes to change shoes and lace up.

First, we would separate the front end from the back end of each skate. Next we would remove the little rubber shock absorbers in order to allow the wheels of our skato to tilt into a curve while racing. Finally, we would attach a sturdy wooden orange crate to the front end of the two-by-four.

Handlebars were made from smaller pieces of wood. We installed a small board across the top of the shelf that was once the strengthening divider when the box held oranges. We carried all our necessities such as knives, cans, sodas, sandwiches, whatever, on the little shelf. We would cruise up and down the neighborhood streets, which were almost devoid of cars and trucks.

As General Claire Chennault made gains in China by shooting down Japanese planes, we armed our skatos with single-shot rubber band guns. We cut up old inner tubes and used the rubber band srips as bullets. The gun was shaped like a real rifle. By stretching the rubber strip from the front of the barrel to a notch-like trip device near the trigger we could fire and reload while doing 9-G pullouts and tight rolls in our fighters.

Unfortunately, as it seems natural with humans, a single-shot rifle soon gave way to more powerful weaponry—the machine gun! We made our machine guns by cutting a dozen notches on the top of the rifle barrel, stretching a cloth tape from the front to the rear, and placing stretched rubber bands from the front to each of the notches. When we pulled the tape, the rubber band bullets would rise up above the notches and fire away. Our guns were both semi- and fully-automatic. If you pulled the tape slowly, the rubber bands would fire one at a time. If you yanked the tape hard, all the bullets would fly out in a devastating fusillade.

As the war seemed to come closer to us, we became less and less satisfied with our old fashioned single, hand-held automatic rubber band rifles. What we needed for our fighter plane skatos were pairs of *mounted* machine guns! We got even longer multi-shot rifles and mounted them to the top of our orange crate skatos. But then another problem became apparent. While executing a sharp turn to get on our enemy's tail, if we took our hands from the wooden handlebars to fire the machine guns, we would lose control and crash.

One of us—I'm not sure who—came up with the brilliant solution of incorporating the two machine guns into the handles. Now we could make sharp turns, train our sights on the enemy's tail, and fire off two bursts of rubber band bullets without losing control of our "plane."

We had originally fashioned tin can lids to simulate headlights but these were removed as we went to war and instead we painted a shark's head on the front of our skatos to strike fear into our enemies. Had I saved the pretty labels on the end of each orange crate I made into skatos, I'd be a rich man today!

An orange crate label from the thirties.

The Butter and Egg Man

I was a nine-year-old butter and egg man. My older brother John used to drive up to Lancaster County in the Amish part of Pennsylvania every Friday afternoon and buy a station-wagon load of butter and eggs.

Every Friday night we would candle the eggs to look for bad ones. The candle was actually a light bulb set behind a piece of cardboard. There was a small, egg-sized and -shaped hole in the cardboard to concentrate the light on the egg. If we saw any dark spots inside the eggs we had to throw them away. By candling our own eggs we got a cheaper price from the farmer; then we could sell them for a few pennies cheaper to our customers.

John saved the rotten eggs for some of his forays into enemy territory. When rotten tomatoes and eggs were traded back and forth rather than bullets from "street sweepers" that are used on the streets today.

I had a small wooden wagon, and on Saturday mornings I would load up a crate of thirty dozen eggs and twenty pounds of fresh homemade country butter and begin my rounds. I had more than twenty customers on my block alone. As I got older I enlarged my sales area by several more blocks, and I often sold as many as three crates in one morning.

John gave me five cents a dozen for delivery and a quarter for every new customer I signed up. After a year or two I went on strike for higher wages. My brother refused to pay and that was the end of the butter and egg business.

The Horseradish Man

Did you ever eat really fresh horseradish? Not the kind you buy in a bottle at the store, but horseradish ground right before your eyes? We ate it often when the horseradish man came around and set up his stand in our alley.

He had a grinder with gears and wheels and a crank-like handle. It was bolted to a four-legged stand and looked something like a high stool with a machine on top. As he came into our alley he would sing out, "Horseradish, horseradish, get your nice, fresh horseradish." He drew out the last part of his song so that the word *horseradish* would be sung for almost a full minute.

Mothers would send their children with a small bowl for a quarter's worth of the red-hot root. The horseradish man would unshoulder his grinder as a bunch of kids anxiously watched and waited. Under the wheels, gears and handle were two drawers. From the large bottom drawer he would pull out a fresh horseradish root about an inch thick and a foot long. As he turned the crank, he would feed the root into the grinder and watch as the right amount dropped into the smaller upper drawer.

He would then empty the small drawer of freshly ground root into the customer's bowl and move on down the alley chanting his horse-radish song. We kids would follow him to the end of block hoping for a taste. We'd beg him for a free sample and he would claim it was too hot for little kids. We would beg him some more, and finally he would search all around in his bottom drawer and come up with a small shred of root for us. He cut it so that however many kids were begging, each would have a piece.

We would run away screaming like chickens who've just gotten a tasty morsel and don't want to share it with the latecomers. But in the end we shared, because that was the rule. Besides, it was too hot for just one person to eat the whole piece.

The Iceman

I always liked to see the iceman come through our alley. He came every day during the summer and two or three times a week during the winter.

During the winters in the mid-thirties, when we were deepest into the Depression, we saved a few dollars a week by using a metal window icebox instead of buying ice. The galvanized metal box was suspended outside our kitchen window. Whenever we wanted anything kept really cold we opened the window and put the food on one of the shelves.

Our iceman didn't seem to mind our avoiding him for a few months each winter. He still came down our alley with his tired old horse and a rickety wagon that squeaked for want of grease. He sat up front on a wooden seat, and his ice filled the back of the wagon. During warm weather he covered the ice with a tattered canvas tarp. The tarp prevented the ice from melting too fast. After our family finances improved a little we went back to the luxury of having an ice box right in our kitchen. No more standing on a low ladder and letting in a blast of cold air whenever we wanted to use the window ice box.

The floor of his wagon was wet, and it had a million splinters from a million stabs with an ice pick. The splinters were like fur on a cat when you stroked it the right way. If you ran your hand the wrong way, the splinters would tickle. The soft splinters would never penetrate your skin. I can still remember the feel in my fingers of the floor of his wagon as I tried to reach a small piece of ice that had broken off a big block.

Every house on our block posted a large card in the window that told the iceman how many pounds to deliver. When the housewife arranged the card with a big "50" on the top, the iceman knew to deliver a fifty-pound block of ice to the house. Without the sign, the iceman would have had to make two trips to the house: one to see if his customer wanted ice and, if so, how much, and a second trip to deliver it.

Our ice man could pull a hundred-pound block of ice from under the tarp with his ice-tongs, throw it onto his leather apron-protected shoulder, and with no apparent effort, carry it up twenty steps. If the order was for less than one hundred pounds, he would stab the block ten or twenty times in a straight line. Finally, he gave the block a hefty stab and split it exactly the way he wanted. The leather apron protected him from both the melting ice and the sharp edges from the recent cut. In the summer, the whole right side of his body would be dripping wet from the melting ice.

Sometimes his customers weren't home. He would deliver the ice anyway if the sign was in the window. He was trusted to enter the

A winter window icebox we used in the thirties.

kitchen and place the block in the large wooden ice boxes we all had in those days. If there was food in the way or a nearly melted chunk of ice, he would move everything around so the new block would set in its proper place. He would then put the food back, clean the wet floor, and close the door after him. No doors were locked; tradesmen always came right into our houses and placed their goods on the table or in the icebox and left.

After the ice was cut up and delivered there were many small chips on the wagon floor. We kids were allowed to climb up and get the small pieces. We sucked them for what seemed like hours.

Often, we would "forget" to get off the wagon and the iceman would "forget" to chase us. After we had ridden several blocks, he would suddenly notice us and holler roughly, "What are you kids doing on my wagon? Get off and run on home!" We'd jump off and run away. We could hear him mutter something about "Damn kids nowadays."

My Mother's Father, Edward Fay

Engine number 54, firehouse at sixty-third and Lancaster Avenue, built by my Grandfather Fay around 1908.

My Grandparents

Contracting must be in my genes. My father and both my grandfathers were builders. My daughter and two sons have construction skills that most young people lack. As my father went on jobs with his father and I went with mine, so too did my children go with me on a job whenever possible. Now my son Teig is teaching my seven-year-old grandson building skills such as stripping wire, sawing wood, and hammering nails.

My mother's father, Edward Fay, was born in Philadelphia about 1838. Edward graduated from Philadelphia Central High School in 1854 and founded the Star Pottery. After building up the business with more than twenty employees, he was wiped out by a tragic fire. He had no insurance. He started over by building porches in West Philadelphia and gradually built his business into a major construction company in the city.

The only building that he built with which I am familiar was the fire house at 63rd and Lancaster Avenue, just across the street from Our Lady of Lourdes School. The firehouse is the home of Engine Company 54. I passed it twice every day for seven years. In the thirties, it had two front doors and a high tower for drying hoses. (The city didn't have hot air blowers to dry out hoses in those days. Instead, after a fire, they hoisted the wet hoses by pulley to the top of a fifty-foot tower and let them drip dry.) Now, there is just one big front door to accommodate the bigger fire engines of today. The firemen use hot air blowers to dry their hoses, and the tower is gone. I went to visit Engine 54 this past summer and it was closed tighter than a drum. It used to be wide open in summer, and the firemen would sit out front or pitch horseshoes in the side yard. They always had a kind word for us kids and let us climb on the engines, and pet their Dalmatian, and even slide down the shiny brass pole or have a mouthful of cool water from their drinking fountain. No more. If they open the doors now, they will lose all the cool air from the air conditioning, so they are pretty much isolated from the community except perhaps for a few rare days in spring and fall.

My mother's mother, Ellen McIlvaine, was born in 1855, also in Philadelphia. She attended St. Anne's Parochial School, at 3rd & Lehigh. A few years ago my sister Jule went to St. Anne's to look up our grandmother's record. She was told by the principal that they didn't keep girl's records in those days. Ellen taught school before she and Edward married in 1875. After she married, she became a milliner, attending New York fashion shows. She would view the latest designs

and retire to the ladies' room to make an illicit sketch. She returned to Philadelphia, where she would sell her fashionable hats for hundreds of dollars. Often they equaled several months' wages each. She had a small but affluent clientele in West Philadelphia.

My father's father, Edward F. Hogan, was born in Tipperary, Ireland, in 1837 and died in Philadelphia in 1892. He came to Philadelphia as a young man. My father's mother was Ella Higgins, born in Liverpool to Irish parents also in 1837. In 1856, my grandfather took off for the gold fields of California. In 1861, he enlisted with Company F, 4th Regi-

My father's mother, Ellen Hogan.

My mother's mother, Ella McIlvane Fay.

ment of the California Infantry Volunteers, Captain Cullam, Commanding. On November 20, 1864, he was discharged at Drum Barracks, California, after serving his three year enlistment. On his discharge papers his profession listed him as an iron monger.

When his enlistment was up, he returned to Philadelphia. Within a few months wanderlust got to him again and he re-enlisted on Saint Patrick's Day in 1865. He took the place of a Quaker who was to be drafted. In the Civil War you could buy out of the draft if you found someone to take your place who wasn't scheduled to be taken. As he had already served his enlistment he "re-upped" and the Quaker gave him $400 for taking his place.

His second enlistment was in Company F, 104th Pennsylvania Infantry, short but not sweet. He was wounded twice, first in a skirmish on March 29, 1865, on the road between Petersburg and Farmville, Virginia. His second wound was more serious. The second finger of his left hand was shot off in action at Sarlon Creek, Virginia, on April 6, 1865, three days before Lee surrendered at Appomattox. He received a pension of five dollars a month. After he died, his widow received six dollars a month.

My grandfather was somewhat like the character "Seldom Seen Smith" in the book *The Monkey Wrench Gang*. He would come home

21. *River Drive Tunnel, Fairmount Park. Philadelphia.*

There is no photo of my father's father, just this postcard of the East River Drive Tunnel he worked on in the nineteenth century.

for short visits and then take off again. He did this eleven times and my grandmother had eleven children, only four of whom survived childhood.

Because of his wanderlust he never had much money or position. One job he had that is proudly told at family gatherings was working on the hand-carved rock tunnel on East River (now Kelly) Drive. According to one story, he was the contractor or superintendent on the job. According to another, he won $100 for being the first laborer to break through to the other side of the tunnel. His wife, my grandmother Hogan, worked in local knitting mills when she was not occupied with her many children.

When Grandmother Fay was just twelve years old her needlepoint of Christ on the Cross won first prize in her class at the Centennial Exposition in Philadelphia in 1876.

Courtesy Temple University Urban Archives

The Lamplighter

Every evening just before dusk, while we were all in our back alley playing roller skate hockey or touch football, the lamplighter would pass our way on his rounds. In the winter his coming would be a sign that dinner was ready. In the summer it was a signal to go inside and prepare for bed.

Our lamplighter was an old man. We never knew his name. He wore a floppy hat, a red neckerchief, and a plaid lumberjacket in both winter and summer. He had a thick, black, drooping mustache and seemed quite mysterious to us. We had all sorts of ideas about him and made up stories about him that amused us for hours after he passed by. A few fathers on our block had been wounded in the Great War, and we imagined that he too had suffered some grave injury or personal tragedy. We had great imaginations.

He wore baggy pants and scuffed shoes and carried a two-piece ladder that tapered at the top so that it fit securely around the lamp post. We had five gas lights in our alley. The huge glass globes were mounted on beautiful cast iron posts and had a crossbar just below the glass so that the lamplighter's ladder had a place to lean when he mounted it.

Sometimes you can see them today as decorations in upscale shopping malls. A large part of Cape May, New Jersey, is still illuminated by the same gas lamps that have been in place for more than a century.

Our lamplighter would stop at each post, unshoulder and assemble his ladder, lean it against the pole, and climb to the top. After he reached the top he would raise the globe, turn on a gas jet, and create a spark with some sort of flintstone device. He would spend a minute or two adjusting the flame to the proper brilliance. Then he would lower the glass, climb down, disassemble his ladder, sling it over his shoulder, and walk to the next light post. We often followed him down the block and watched him light each lamp. None of us kids ever said a word, nor did he ever talk to us. We just watched.

It wasn't until I was six or seven that I realized that he also came around very early in the morning to extinguish the lights. In the summer, sometimes when I awoke early, I would wait for him to come by. Then I knew it was time for me to get up.

When I was about ten, the city discovered that it was cheaper to keep the lights on all the time rather than pay a crew of lamplighters to turn the lamps on and off; they restructured and downsized the department. I never saw him again.

Mr. Abbott

I must have been ten years old before I realized that, though he was delivering Abbott's Milk, our milkman's name was not Abbott. I still called him Mr. Abbott and he never seemed to mind.

Usually Mr. Abbott made his deliveries so early in the morning that I was still asleep. Sometimes I made myself get up before sunrise just so I could greet him. He knew every kid on the block by his or her first name and always had a kind word for each of us.

In the summer, Mr. Abbott would walk right into our house and put the bottles of milk in our icebox. He would even rearrange the food so that his milk would be right next to the block of ice. During the winter, when there was no fear that the milk would go bad by sitting outside for a few hours until we got up, he would leave the milk on the small landing by our back door. If it was really cold, the milk would freeze and push the cream up over the cardboard lid. I don't think there was any such thing as homogenized milk then, never mind skim milk and low fat milk. Sometimes, my mother would let me take small bites of the frozen cream.

Every two weeks or so, Mr. Abbott would stop by in the afternoon with his horse and wagon to chat awhile, collect money, or deliver special orders of butter or cream. His horse knew every house along the route, so Mr. Abbott could just walk along our alley and his horse would follow. Every few houses he would refill his small carriers, each holding eight quart bottles of milk, and drop them off at his customers' houses. As he returned through the garden gates, he would give a short, high-pitched whistle. The horse knew that was the signal to catch up. We kids often tried to get the horse to start or stop by trying to imitate Mr. Abbott's special whistle, but we could never fool the horse. He listened only to his master.

When we were older, about eleven or twelve, we sometimes walked two or three miles to the Abbott's horse barn to watch Mr. Abbott clean and feed his friend. Once in a while, our milkman would pass us a damaged quart of ice cream with spoons he always seemed to have in his pocket. We would crawl into an empty stall and gorge ourselves on the finest ice cream ever made, with the possible exception of our own homemade ice cream. I don't know if it was the best store-bought ice cream ever. I guess it tasted better because it was a gift from our friend, Mr. Abbott.

It wasn't until a few years ago that my sister Jule told me that our Mr. Abbott had a college degree. It was in the middle of the Depression and I guess Mr. Abbott felt lucky he even had a job.

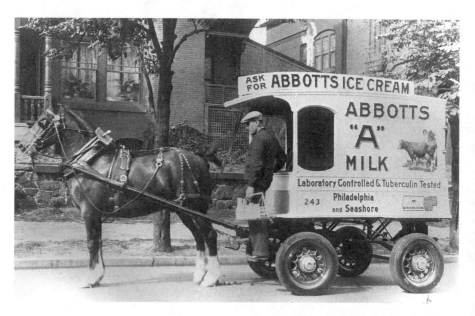

Courtesy of Temple University Urban Archives

The Rag and Junk Man

Our rag and junk man not only bought scrap iron and aluminum, but rags and old newspapers as well. He wouldn't turn down bottles or anything of value. Of course he never got the bottles we collected, which had a two-cent deposit value on them. Still, he must have had a market for glass because he would give us a penny for ten or more bottles without deposit value.

His cargo of junk was eclectic and his wagon defied the laws of nature. One wheel was so wobbly we always watched to see if it would come off. It never did. His Dobbin was just as rickety. I forget his name but he was a loyal horse who would follow his master up our alley without the use of reigns to urge him on.

The junk wagon was always overloaded with broken pots and pans, bent bicycle frames and wheels, buckets of rusty nuts and bolts, pieces of iron or steel broken off cars, wagons, and old kitchen stoves. As cast iron stoves and pipes brought the most money there was always a pile of that precious commodity aboard.

Our rag and junk man came by every Thursday afternoon and we kids were always waiting for him with some sort of scrap material that he would buy. We were never lucky enough to come across old cast iron radiators. They brought nearly ten cents a pound. The grownups cornered that market as a hundred-pound radiator could fetch ten dollars, more than a day's pay. Even more prized was copper in pot

Courtesy of the Pennsylvania Historical Society

The rag man loaded down with newspapers, bed springs and junk shouting his song in West Philadelphia.

or wire form, and car engine blocks that required two or three men to load them into the junk wagon.

We were paid a good price for aluminum foil. We'd spend all spring walking the streets of our neighborhood looking for empty cigarette packs that had thin aluminum foil glued to thin paper. We would spend hours every week peeling the foil from the paper and rolling it into ever bigger balls of foil. By the time summer came around and we needed extra quarters for the swimming pool and dimes for the Saturday matinee, we'd have balls nearly a foot in diameter and weighing twenty or thirty pounds. At twelve cents a pound we'd have earned two or three dollars for our three months work.

An added bonus was the tobacco we found and saved from the thousands of butts also lying in the gutters. We bought a cigarette roller for a dollar and papers for a dime and we all had as many cigarettes to smoke as we could stand, which wasn't very many.

Selling old newspapers was less profitable than selling junk but it was more reliable. We each had our favorite list of neighbors who saved papers for us. They never bothered to wait for the junk man and we would collect their papers every few days and pile them in our garages.

Often, we'd have several hundred pounds of old newspapers neatly bound waiting for his wagon to come rattling down our alley. Our rag and junk man had a scale hanging out over the back of his wagon and after weighing each bundle of papers, and after adding them up gave us a dollar or two for our labors.

Like most of the people who passed through our alley collecting or selling, he had a distinctive cry "Rags, any old rags . . . I buy rags . . . I buy junk . . . Rag Man, Rag Man . ." would echo up and down the alley, and dozens of kids would drag out their treasured horde and sit by their pile waiting to bargain with the rag and junk man.

I still save newspapers, cans, aluminum foil, and bottles, but no longer get reimbursed when I take a truckload to the local recycling depot. There are no deposit laws in Pennsylvania now so those containers that aren't turned in just litter our roads and landscape from the Ohio line to the Delaware River.

My Little Red Wagon

I can't tell my psychiatrist that I never had a little red wagon like the other kids on my block. So I can't use that as an excuse for whatever pitfalls I've encountered as an adult. I always had a little red wagon. Well, not really always, but I well remember my first one. I got it for Christmas. I had wanted one desperately almost since I could walk—certainly for as far back as I can remember.

A few months before my fourth or fifth Christmas, I began my campaign. I was very, very good and did almost everything I was told. At the annual Gimbels Thanksgiving Day Parade in Philadelphia I even mailed a special delivery letter to Santa Claus. I know it went directly to the North Pole because there were two clowns in the parade who pushed huge mail boxes on wheels alongside Santa's sleigh on the parade route.

It was so special a delivery that you didn't even have to put stamps on the envelope. As soon as the parade was over Santa Claus would read all those special delivery letters. I was sure that my letter would be one of the first he read. The clown postman assured me that the letters would accompany Santa that very night when he returned to the North Pole. Even though I tried to be extra good between Thanksgiving and Christmas, I was perhaps guilty of being smug, so positive was I that I'd get my wish.

Up before dawn on Christmas Day, down the stairs, and sure enough, Santa had kept his promise—or rather, met my request.

Encircled with a big green ribbon was my little red wagon parked next to the tree.

It was cold and raining that morning and I wasn't allowed to take the wagon outside for a test spin down our block-long sidewalks, so my sister Jule helped me carry the wagon to our L-shaped basement. Then we took turns pushing each other at breakneck speed from the big room at the front of the house down a narrow hall past the furnace room and into the much smaller laundry room. There we'd make high-speed U-turns on two wheels and race back to the big front room again.

I don't remember if the object of the game was to see if we could knock each other off the speeding wagon or just see how fast we could go—but roll over we often did. The scars are gone but the memory of our own private Indy 500 lingers.

As I grew older I used the wagon for both work and play. I filled it with rocks to help my father terrace our gardens. I collected old newspapers up and down the block to sell to the rag and junk man when he came down our back alley with his special street cry, "Rags, old rags . . . I buy old rags." At eight or nine, I was old enough to pull my wagonload of old newspapers to the ragman's place of business about five blocks from my house, thus making a few more pennies per load.

When I was eleven or twelve I worked for my older brother John by using the wagon to deliver butter and eggs around the neighborhood. But that's another story (see "The Butter and Egg Man").

I soon moved up to the exalted ranks of supermarket delivery boy. That's where the real money was. The A&P was just a few blocks away at 62nd Street and Lancaster Avenue. Few people had cars in the thirties. It would never occur to anyone to take a shopping cart home and push it into the nearest gutter after using it. So there was a great demand for our services, especially on Friday evening and all day Saturday. Pennsylvania Blue Laws kept markets closed on Sundays in those days!

We could load three or four heavy paper bags full of groceries in our wagons—almost ten dollars' worth of food for our richer customers. By that time I had a fancy stake-body wagon. It was built more for heavy-duty utility work than mere play—pretty much like the red 1992 Ford 250 pickup I drive today.

We usually got a minimum of ten cents for delivering a wagonload of groceries a few blocks. Even though we had no meters we expected the tip to escalate five cents for each block past the few-block limit.

We delivery boys had our own rules. We took our turns in a wagon rank much as taxis do today at airports. Of course we had our favorite customers and we could jump the line if our own special Mrs. Bigbucks wanted us over others.

We knew who the good tippers were as well as the poor ones. We knew who lived up a steep hill or had several flights of steps in an apartment house. We didn't mind so much the people who lived in apartment houses if there was an elevator on site. Even though the trip might take a little longer it was always fun to ride up and down to the top floor a few times after we delivered the bags and got our tip. Of course, just before we got off, we pushed every button in the elevator.

The poor tippers quickly got a bad reputation and we would always be occupied reading a comic book when Mrs. Cheapskate finished paying her bill at the checkout counter and called for a wagon. Joe Dougherty, the store manager, kept a semblance of order and in case no one wanted to carry Mrs. C's groceries, he'd designate one of us to do it. He tried to be fair in assigning us those no-pay or "two-cookie" jobs so we all took turns with the losers. He knew the poor tippers, too, and would tell the skinflint customer that we were not carrying groceries for fun but to earn money.

One of us, whose name I won't reveal here, when given two cookies for a six-block trek, dumped all of Mrs. Cheapskate's groceries on the floor. It was the middle of the Depression and we needed cash to go to the movies and buy baseball and war cards. Our parents had no money to send us to the movies and the Overbrook Theater wouldn't accept cookies in lieu of cash. Besides, Mr. Dougherty would always give us bags of broken cookies he couldn't sell. He kept the label for reimbursement and it was a nice arrangement.

When Mrs. Cheapskate complained that not only did we all refuse to carry her bags, but that one of us actually dumped her groceries on the floor, Mr. Dougherty told her a few facts of life—that we could not use cookies to buy the important necessities of our early teenage lives. He told her that we worked for money and that he gave us all the cookies we could eat. After the lecture she became a fair tipper but we still didn't fight to see who would carry her bags.

Our hero who dumped the grocery bags later became a real hero by wining the Silver Star and Purple Heart at Normandy. I have to tell my psychiatrist that I can't even remember whatever happened to my little red wagon.

When I was fifteen, I lied about my age and got an after-school job as a checker at the same A&P. It was wartime so Mr. Dougherty didn't ask for proof of my age. He was glad to hire anyone at fifty cents an hour, under age or not.

Fifty-five years later, my brother Ed sent me a brand new red wagon. This one was made in China.

My Friend Bobby Thompson

Bobby Thompson was my first friend. He's still a friend, although I only seem to see him every ten years when our 1941 class of Our Lady of Lourdes School in Overbrook meets.

He lived across the alley and down about fifteen or twenty houses. We played in the water-filled ditches in the broken alley's pavement when we were four or five years old. As we grew older the broken concrete was replaced by a beautiful new pavement of smooth, clean concrete. The new paving arrived at about the same time we were able to navigate on roller skates. We played roller skate hockey, crack the whip, and toboggan skating where we all got in a line and went as fast as we could up and down the 408-foot alley.

Bobby's father, who recently died at the age of ninety-six, was president of Thompson Carpet Company. He was a sergeant in France in the First World War and fought in the Battle of Argonne. He left nine children, thirty grandchildren, and twenty-nine great-grandchildren. When we were growing up he worked just a few blocks from our homes. One time he brought home several very large, sturdy wood shipping crates. Each box was about five feet square and four feet high. We stacked a few on top of each other and several more next to each other. That way we created a five- or six-room clubhouse. We cut out windows and doorways and had a great time holding secret meetings, wolfing down sandwiches, and playing lord of the manor.

To improve communications, Bobby and I built our own closed-circuit phone system with strong string and tin cans. We waxed the string by running it through a candle and secured it through little holes in the bottom of each can. The bottom of the can acted like a diaphragm and the vibrations of our voices would clearly carry back and forth between our houses. In order to make up for the sag in the 300-foot line, we operated from our rear second story bedroom windows. Even then we had to have a very taut line so that trucks and envious playmates wouldn't snag it and tear it down. Our voices were quite clear, better than some phone conversations I've had recently on Ma Bell's machine or whoever is running the local phone system this week. I don't remember what we talked about but it was very important.

Bobby was the youngest of his eight siblings. I was the youngest of five. We had a lot in common and walked to school together every day for the seven years we went to Our Lady of Lourdes School.

Sometimes we worked together on my tree house. My father was a friend of Philip Nowlan, the author-artist of *Buck Rogers in the Twenty-Fifth Century.* Mr. Nowlan lived nearby in Bala and every so often we would visit him and his children. They had an aerial cable car that ran between two tree houses. I couldn't manage a cable car until I built one for my own children thirty years later, but it sure made a big impression on me at the time. I'm still a Buck Rogers fan.

Marie Keenan helps her brother John answer the phone.

Puppets

When the Depression deepened in the early thirties, my father took advantage of his hobbies and turned them into money-making enterprises. One such hobby was puppets and marionettes. A puppet (from the Latin *pupa,* "doll") is manipulated from below the stage by a hand inserted under the puppet's skirt. The middle finger and thumb are inserted into the two arms and the index finger into the head. A marionette (from the French, "Little Mary") is managed by strings that connect the limbs and head to an X-shaped rack manipulated by a person above and behind the stage. Simple marionettes have five strings while more complex ones can have as many as seven or nine. With both forms, there is always a great deal of head movement and arms and legs flying every which way.

My father first became interested in puppets when he saw a street show in Florence, Italy, where the first Punch and Judy performance is supposed to have taken place. This was on one of the family's trips to Europe before I was born. It seemed we always had puppets, and my father would often entertain us while he carved and fashioned the puppets. My mother was the seamstress and made all the costumes as well as playing the female roles in our shows.

My father would negotiate with a school to put on a performance. The children were each expected to pay ten cents, and my father would usually split the take with the school. I remember once he played at my school, Our Lady of Lourdes. I was very proud to know that my father was the Sol Hurok of West Philadelphia. We often played two shows a day, one in the afternoon for the children and another at night for the parents. On a really good day, we would have as many as two hundred guests. That would net the school and our family ten dollars each. Our share was enough for a week's groceries if we spent wisely.

Before one of these school performances we would have a dress rehearsal in our large basement combination theater and playroom, where my father had constructed two stages, one for puppets and one for marionettes. The one designed for puppets was in the form of a triptych made of three large canvas paintings, each four feet wide and seven feet high. The center canvas contained the main stage area for the puppets and on each side panel there was a tiny stage with a small door for the interlocutor to have his say before each performance. Interlocutors were also popular during the riverboat minstrel show era of the last century. Then, they were usually politically incorrect actors in blackface like Al Jolson in a later era. In any event, the puppet show interlocutors helped the children to understand what they were about to see on the stage.

The other stage consisted of a score of half-inch steel pipes that my father would screw together to make a stage about eight feet wide by seven feet high and perhaps four feet deep. This stage was for marionettes. When the pipes were all screwed together he would drape them with bright red satin cloth. The stage was about three feet off the floor and the front could be drawn apart like a real stage curtain.

My father's Little Red Riding Hood marionette show.

My father's repertory included the basic *Punch and Judy*, *Little Red Riding Hood*, and *The Gingham Dog and the Calico Cat*. I still remember some of the lines when the cat and dog had their fight and the Chinese plate sat on the mantelpiece and watched the scrap between the animated stuffed animals. I also seem to remember the crocodile eating Punch at the end of the show while all the children clapped approval. Or perhaps it might be a wolf eating Little Red Riding Hood's grandmother. Some monster was always eating the good guy and then getting his or her comeuppance in the end. I don't remember a puppet play that didn't somehow end violently. Perhaps our fascination with violence can be traced back to children's nursery rhymes and puppet shows.

Naturally, the children loved to watch Punch beat Judy with a stick. But the screaming young audience didn't appreciate it when Punch started to beat his babies as well, and they cheered when the police took him away. Punch was always hunchbacked and had a long hooked nose. Somehow he escaped from jail and fled with his dog, Toby. The violence of the story was balanced by its wit and humor. Lord knows how many protest groups would picket such a show today.

As a young man my father was a spear carrier in the Philadelphia Opera Company for many, many years, so show business was in his blood. I don't think he ever sang on stage, but at home I often heard his renditions from various operas and his parody of the Toreador song from *Carmen:* "Oh Theodora, don't spit on the flora, use the cuspidora; what d'ya think it's fora?" When I was only four or five, before things fell apart, my father would don his tuxedo and my mother would dress to the nines with rings and necklaces, and every Friday evening during the season, they would attend the opera in their reserved box.

I had a birthday party when I was four or five and all the neighborhood kids were invited. We had a big birthday layer cake baked by my mother. She would wrap pennies and nickels in wax paper and bake the coins into the cake. As the birthday boy I got the slice with a quarter while my guests got only one- or five-cent prizes.

The main event of the party was a show by a beautiful midget. All of us were assembled in the living room. The doorway to the dining room was curtained off like a familiar puppet stage. Our great big wind-up Gramophone with thick records began a song, the curtain opened, and this beautiful full-faced lady, all painted up with lipstick and rouge, with a tiny body and tiny arms and legs, began to dance and sing. She was real! And she knew me, and performed a special musical number written just for me. I could not believe it.

Immediately after the song, I ran upstairs looking for my mother to tell her about the incredible show I had just witnessed. I could find her nowhere for about ten minutes until she appeared in the kitchen. I told her that she just missed the most wonderful show with a beautiful, tiny woman who sang just as she did! Mother was so sorry she missed the show. It wasn't until years later that I discovered the headless rag doll in a long-forgotten trunk.

A Misspent Youth

Even as little children, we indulged in all sorts of gambling. Pitch penny, marbles, bottle top pitching, mumblety-peg, and card flipping and tossing were the most popular of our gambling games.

Whenever we had a few spare pennies we started a game of pitching them against a wall or a bottom step. The person whose penny came closest to the wall won the pot. I won and lost many a fortune (anything over ten cents was a fortune) at that game. Unlike the more simple game of heads or tails, pitching pennies required considerable adroitness, and a few of my friends seemed to have a lock on that particular skill, often winning as much as a quarter each week at their nefarious trade.

I didn't much like playing heads or tails with pennies or playing cards because it went too fast and required the assistance of luck rather than a developed skill. You could lose your fortune in less than a minute if luck wasn't with you that day. I had more faith in my skill than in luck.

◆ Marbles ◆

Marbles was a great game of skill. We drew a circle in the dirt about two feet in diameter and put two or more marbles in the center, depending upon how many of us were playing. The object was to try to knock the encircled marbles out of the ring and thus win the target marble. We each had our favorite marbles and they came in all colors,

A 1930s marble tournament open to boys and girls.

designs, and sizes. We also had giant marbles that we never played but kept as prized possessions.

Another variation of marble shooting was to dig a small hole about two inches deep and in diameter in the middle of the circle. Whoever was first to flick a marble into the hole won the other marbles in the circle.

Had I kept all the marbles I won, I'd be a rich man today as they have increased in value a thousand or more times. Collections are now in most of the children's museums around the country. Some are available at the numerous old toy and collectibles shows I attend, but the price is beyond me.

I read recently that in the twenties, the Akro Agate Company, a marble manufacturer in West Virginia, employed over 125 workers to make more than two million marbles a week. They went out of business in 1951.

◆ War Cards ◆

After a year's nationwide search I finally tracked down a baker's dozen of war cards from the thirties for which I paid $65. I once had a complete set of all 240 bubble gum "Horrors of War" cards that were produced by GUM, Inc. in Philadelphia. Each card depicted a scene from one of the wars going on at the time. The cards described events from the Japanese invasion of Manchuria and, later, China, the Spanish Civil War, and the Italian invasion of Ethiopia, with its gruesome comment by a bomber pilot who likened the exploding bodies to the "blooming of a beautiful red rose." There were other clashes around the globe which have slipped my mind and perhaps eluded the history books. These cards bring back memories of the horrors of war in the thirties when big nations went after little ones with ruthless abandon. Things haven't changed much.

The events were all vividly described on the cards with a full color picture on the front and the accompanying story on the back. Many of the battles were illustrated and described, from the "Rape of Nanking" where more civilians were raped, bayoneted, and shot by the Japanese invaders in just one insane weekend than were killed in the bombing of Hiroshima, to the pointless aerial bombardment of Addis Ababa where the only targets were civilians. At the bottom of each card was printed the exhortation, "To know the HORRORS OF WAR is to want PEACE."

Aside from tossing and flipping them, the cards taught us, albeit in a slanted fashion, current history. The front of card #53 depicted the Japanese bombing of the gunboat USS *Panay* while on patrol in the Yangtze River on December 12, 1937, four years minus five days before the attack on Pearl Harbor. The first bomb to hit the *Panay* (the ship was named after one of the Philippine Islands) wounded the captain as he stood on the bridge. The blast flung him against the wheel, rendering him unconscious. Command was immediately passed to Lieutenant Andes, who directed antiaircraft machine gun fire against the attackers. The playing cards, lacking political correctness, referred to the enemy as Japs.

Card #135 depicted and described a street battle from a rooftop in Barcelona. The card clearly favored the Republicans, who were shown firing down on Franco's better-armed forces in the street. In answer to my and my schoolmates' sister-mandated daily prayers at Our Lady of Lourdes School for Franco's victory, the Republicans lost the civil war. I wonder if there was ever a congressional investigation into that form of propaganda.

While my friends also collected baseball cards, I was more interested in global events. I never took from my original complete set of war cards and gambled and traded only with spares and extras. I remember trading as many as ten extra war cards for just one that I lacked to help fill my collection. I rarely flipped cards but rather relied on my "tossing" skill by more often than not tossing my card closer to the wall than my opponent's, thus winning their card.

The five dollars each that I paid for the cards I recently bought works out to a price increase of 50,000 percent over fifty-seven years!

Front and back of "Horrors of War" bubble gum trading cards.

I haven't the foggiest idea whatever happened to my really priceless original collection.

Not long ago I read that during World War I 10 percent of the casualties were civilian and 90 percent were military. In World War II, it was 50-50; and in what was once Yugoslavia, as well as Rwanda and a dozen other countries around the world, the casualty rate is now less than 1 percent military and over 99 percent civilian.

◆ Bottle Caps ◆

I imagine that I played "bottle caps" before I got into war cards and marbles. Bottle caps were free for the picking and it was with those that I honed my tossing, pitching, and flipping skills. Rather than "knuckling" them up close to a wall, we usually drew a chalk line on the pavement. With a wall, one could mistakenly nudge the opponent's bottle cap closer to the wall and thus lose. With a chalk line, we would strive to knock the opponent's bottle cap further away from the other side of the line and thus win. As bottle caps held very little real value, it was the least favorite of our games of skill.

As our skills increased so did our special tricks. We would rub a bottle cap back and forth on a concrete sidewalk to scrape off the paint so that it would slide further and with greater control. We even filled them with candle wax and ultimately with lead to give them more weight so they could better push the opponent's cap out of the game.

◆ Mumblety-Peg ◆

Every one of us had a jackknife, and when we weren't whittling or throwing them at tree trunks we spent many hours seeing who was most skillful at mumblety-peg. We would toss our knives so the blade stuck in the ground. The skill requirement increased as the game progressed. The first round would always be a simple throwing of the knife to the ground so that it stuck in an upright position. On the next toss, you had to make the knife do a complete flip before it stuck. We would then progress to balancing the knife blade on a finger tip, then the back of the hand, then the elbow or knee before allowing it to fall and stick in the ground.

As the challenge increased, some of us would be eliminated when our knives fell over or failed to stick in the ground. The competition became really tough when we had to flip the knives unseen from behind our backs to the ground. Whoever was last to misfire won the game.

I don't think we gambled on these tosses. The satisfaction of just winning a demanding skill game was enough.

As a fledging rower for the Penn Athletic Club on the Schuylkill River, Philadelphia. 1940.

My Fifteen Minutes of Fame

It was the summer of 1940. I had just turned thirteen and was in training as a raw recruit coxswain for the Penn Athletic Club in Philadelphia. My boat was the most junior eight-oared shell in the club. I fell into the sport naturally, as my three older brothers had preceded me at the helm.

The 1940 GOP presidential nominating convention was taking place just a mile from our boat house on the Schuylkill River. The City went all out to entertain the free-spending conventioneers, and one of the events was a demonstration boat race along the Avenue of Statues on East River Drive. (It's now called John B. Kelly Drive, named after the great Diamond Sculls champion and father of actress Grace Kelly.) The boat race featured three eight-oared shells. Since it was just a demonstration race and would have no effect on the club's ranking, the club directors thought it was a good opportunity for us neophytes to be in a race with no consequences if we lost.

Our boat won, and the delegates gave us a proper cheer as we slowly rowed over to the temporary platform by the grandstand. As coxswain, it was my job to accept the huge silver trophy cup from Mayor Lamberton. The honored guest, Republican presidential candidate Wendell Willkie, was standing next to the mayor. Even though I was a loyal Democrat, I was still awed by the plethora of Republican dignitaries, from the governor on down to local ward leaders.

News cameras flashed to record for posterity Mayor Lamberton awarding me the trophy. I happily got back into my coxswain's seat for the mile-long row back to our boat house. Aglow with pride, I deftly steered the long shell homeward, beating the slow cadence of a victorious crew much like the drummer on an ancient Greek trireme after sinking a Phoenician warship. I made a perfect docking by the slip, bringing the stern around to gently meet the floating dock. I was met by a small delegation of people I never saw before and was relieved of the cup so that I could safely climb out of the shell.

As I got out of my coxswain's seat in the stern, custom prevailed. As the winning cox, I was grabbed by the crew and given the old one, two, three, and a toss into the dirty Schuylkill River.

I was proud of the symbolic dunking, and after climbing back onto the slip, I gave the proper sequence of commands to my crew to lift, carry, and stow the shell on the rack inside the boat house. Only then did I go looking for our cup. It was not to be seen. When I asked one of the men where it was, he looked at me as though I was a bit daft. "It's back in the safe where it belongs, what do you want with it?" At an early age I learned what a "photo op" is.

Neither Jack Kelly, who was then the most famous Democrat in the city, nor his daughter Grace, with whom I was enamored at the time, managed to attend that particular club celebration. I imagine the Democratic Kellys were being politically correct by avoiding a Republican show.

I don't even have a copy of the historic photograph of the award ceremony to look at. So much for my fifteen minutes of fame.

Born Again

I was born again one cool November Friday evening in 1939. One might call it an intellectual bolt of lightning. It certainly wasn't a slow awakening as to what was right and what was wrong, what was moral and amoral.

No one, I imagine, is ever completely free from prejudices and bigotry, but I like to think I'm pretty close. John Donne said, "No man is an island," and Martin Luther King said, "No one is free until we are all free." But yet, I think one can get pretty close to freedom within oneself even with the rest of the world enslaved.

Early on, I had learned that we Catholics were the "Chosen." The nuns taught me that anyone who wasn't a Catholic, who didn't regularly attend mass and go to confession, had a direct nonstop ticket to Hell. Presbyterians, Baptists, Lutherans were all non-Catholics and thus sinners. There wasn't a particle of difference among them. We didn't credit the Jewish Moses with delivering the Ten Commandments. I just assumed that one of the Catholic Apostles thought them up. We were taught that we should live by those rules, but we didn't always practice what was preached.

Every day we prayed for Franco's victory in Spain. I had a vague impression that Hitler and Mussolini were helping poor Franco in his fight for his form of liberation from the heretical Republicans, but it didn't bother me too much. Like most of my friends, I went along with anti-Negro songs and anti-Jewish jokes. I got to calling my Jewish

Once a warehouse, then a synagogue, and now an apartment house on Upland Way in Wynnefield.

friends Rabbi and the name came back and I was stuck with that nickname for a good part of my youth.

On Halloween in 1939, I dressed up as Hitler complete with hair plastered over my forehead, short Charlie Chaplin mustache, swastika armband, and jack boots. Most of my neighbors thought my costume was great, but not the Paperman family. They gave me candy like the rest of the neighbors but they didn't comment on my costume. It was a few years before I realized why. I still, to this day, wonder why my mother allowed me to dress in such a manner. But she was sick much of the time and had little control or supervision over my activities.

On the Friday night that I was born again, I had gone out looking for excitement with my pals. We wandered over to Wynnefield, a mostly Jewish neighborhood across the Pennsylvania Railroad tracks from my neighborhood, Overbrook.

We came upon a partially built synagogue that was almost complete. It was an ordinary sort of commercial building on Upland Way. It had no towers or stained glass windows, and but for the small sign out front it could have been mistaken for a warehouse. We went up to the door and peeked through a large hole where the lock had not yet been installed. We watched the people worshipping their God and snickered. As we left, I put my mouth to the hole and shouted in, "You goddamn Jews." We all ran away although I don't think we were chased. We laughed a bit at our daring.

Then I began to think. "What if a Jew did the same to us when we were at mass at Our Lady of Lourdes?" That was my awakening—then and there. I began to question a church that allowed me to learn such things. I began to question the rightness of praying for Franco and, by guilty association, for Hitler. When I was kept back in seventh grade, I left the Church and the Catholic school I had attended and went on to eighth grade at Judge Dimner Beeber Junior High School in, of all places, Wynnefield. There I made friends with both Jews and Protestants and my horizons expanded.

Occasional prejudices still pop up in me now and then. Not for individual people, but for those who foster ethnic cleansing, fundamentalists of all stripes, political correctness advocates, etc. Despite the "achievements" of the Nazis in their Aryan purity campaign in the thirties, I think as many people are being killed around the world over religion today as were then. But what do I know?

Courtesy of Temple University Urban Archives

The Snowball Man

Our nearby convenience store sells slush for about a dollar a cup. Only one flavor is offered. I tried it a few years ago, took one sip or bite, and threw the rest away.

In the thirties we didn't have to hop in our car and drive to a convenience store to get a snowball. Back then the snowball man came to us. That was convenience. The snowball man made his daily rounds with his big block of ice and his twenty-flavor laden pushcart. During the dog days of August, he might come through our back alley two or three times in a single afternoon.

Sometimes both the pretzel man and the snowball man were outside our school at lunch and dismissal times from early spring to late fall. The pretzel man was there in winter too.

The snowball man's pushcart held a hundred-pound block of ice that he covered with a light canvas to retard melting. He used this metal scraper to shave "snow" from the ice block. He sold two-, three-, and five-cent paper cups of snow. We stood in line and stated our need that was really dictated by the amount of money we had. It was sort of a child's Peter Principle of the thirties: "The need or thirst expands to meet the number of pennies you have to spend."

After deciding what size snow cone we could afford we then had the luxury of choosing from about twenty flavors. Today's mini-market slush buckets come in one flavor, cherry, like it or lump it! We always asked for our snowball man to shake more flavor onto the top of the cone than he appeared to want to do. In retrospect, I think he purposely held back, anticipating our request for more flavor. Thus he gave no more than he could afford, we got more than we bargained for, and everyone was happy. Some of us would even dare to ask for two flavors on the same cone, and we were usually indulged.

The snowball man would uncover the ice and pick up his box-like scraper. As he pushed it over the block, the flaked ice would build up in the shaver. He would then pack it in the paper cup and douse the cone with colorful and tasty syrup. Unlike the finely crushed sand-like particles of today's slush, our snow was composed of thick flakes. These ice flakes lasted longer than slush, and we could savor the flavor longer.

Today's slush bucket comes with a thick straw so you can suck the mixture out of the plastic container. It was impossible to suck the ice flakes of our cones through a straw.

Sometime near the end of my childhood, the Philadelphia Health Department decided it was unsanitary to have a tarp-covered block of ice in a pushcart and put all the snowball men out of business!

Dimner Beeber Junior High School

Dimner and Dumbner was not such a bad school. I decided to enter the eighth grade there in 1940 after I flunked seventh grade at Our Lady of Lourdes School. I was not going to repeat a year at that institution! I had the full approval of my mother to leave the parochial school. In the sixth grade at Lourdes, I had the highest IQ and the lowest grades

in my class. My mother knew I was smart, the nuns knew I was smart, and I knew I was smart. After my mother died on November 17, 1941, I began the short road to agnosticism, and the Church and I soon parted company.

My sister Jule went all the way through public school. When she was taking tutoring in preparation for her confirmation, Sister Celestine, at Our Lady of Lourdes, whacked her knuckles with a hardwood twelve-inch ruler, the kind that had twelve different species of wood in the stock. Jule didn't have her hands folded in prayer the right way so she got punished. She was just seven or eight and complained bitterly to my mother. She didn't want to go back but our mother talked her into it.

When it happened a second time, Jule just ran home and told mother that if this was the way nuns treated little kids she didn't want to be a Catholic. This time my mother had to bribe my sister to go back once more. She was never hit again, became confirmed, remained a Catholic until she reached maturity, and left the Church. So much for love and understanding.

While I'm on the subject, I just learned the other day from my sister that the same thing happened to my father over a century ago! He was in third grade at a Catholic school at the time. One child had misbehaved, so the nun lined up all the children in the class and banged each one on the head with a heavy geography book, innocent and guilty alike. My father ran home, and his mother pulled him out of the parochial school and sent him to public school to complete his elementary school education.

The interesting thing in these three accounts is that in those days, fifty and a hundred years ago, the nuns could do no wrong and 99.99 percent of parents would approve of whatever torture the nuns chose to inflict on children. Not so with my parents and grandparents. My own children missed that bit of scholastic reinforcement and encouragement in their lives and my grandchildren will also miss it.

While in class at Lourdes, more often than not I would be reading a geography book when I was supposed to be doing sums or looking up a part of history I was more interested in than what was being taught at the time. I was never excessively fond of reading my catechism. Once, I think it was in the sixth grade, our teacher caught me reading the wrong book, tore it out of my hands, and ripped it in two. "Now, have your parents buy you a new book," was her only comment.

I had good friends at Our Lady of Lourdes and still see them at class reunions. Grade school friends certainly have as much or more influence on your future as those from later in life.

Most of the kids at Beeber were Jewish. We didn't even bother going to school on their high holidays. The second largest ethnic group was Italian, and I guess I fell in with everyone else.

My Latin teacher, Mrs. Barrett, was horrible. The first day of class, she walked up and down the aisles predicting who would make it and who would fail: "You will fail, you will pass, you will pass, you will fail." My failure was predicted and it almost came to pass. My mother died two months after school started, on November 17, 1941. There was no recognition of that fact by Mrs. Barrett, or anyone else for that matter. I stayed out of school for a week and had to work twice as hard when I went back. Come to think of it, the nuns at Our Lady of Lourdes weren't too interested in my parents' illnesses either. I don't ever recall any teacher, nun or lay, asking about my parents much less making a home visit.

Flash cards like our wooden airplane identification models

At Beeber, I liked shop the best. Mr. Toll taught electric shop and there I learned the basics of electricity and could soon wire lamps and run simple circuits. I forget my metal shop teacher's name, but the class had all sorts of tinsmithing tools, from brakes to make neat bends in the tin sheet to shears for cutting straight to soldering irons for putting everything together with professional workmanship.

Soon after Pearl Harbor, which was just three weeks after my mother died, our wood shop went to war. We carved small wooden models of airplanes for the government. They were used to help train air raid wardens and soldiers who were to man antiaircraft batteries how to identify both enemy and friendly planes. After we carved them to exacting standards, we would paint them black so they would appear as silhouettes against a dimly lit skyline. We carved Stukas, P-40s, Zeros, and Mitsubishis. I soon grew to recognize in less than a second almost any plane flying as our instructor flashed a light on them to show us how important our work was.

We felt that we were helping the war effort in many other ways, from collecting aluminum pans and tin cans to saving grease and turning it in to the A&P where it would eventually be made into ammunition so that our boys would come home victorious.

Mr. Dubrow was our gym teacher and he took no nonsense from us. Whoever got out of line or acted smart would get a good whack on the backside with a rubber hose. It left no mark but sure did sting. We wouldn't think of complaining to our parents who would most likely add another whack or two for good measure. Today Mr. Dubrow would have been in jail for child abuse. I didn't then, and don't now, feel that he was unfair or abusive.

When we didn't brown-bag it, we usually bought lunch in the cafeteria. A hot dog with sauerkraut was five cents, half a pint of real whole milk was three cents. Good, thick soup was five cents. Dessert was either Jello or some kind of cake and cost a nickel. We never spent over twenty cents for a good hot lunch.

At assembly we sang all sorts of war songs honoring the men and women in the military. I still remember the words to some of them: "Angels of Mercy," which honored the nurses; the Army Air Corps song; the Marines' Hymn; "Over There"; and "Anchors Aweigh." The Coast Guard song, I am ashamed to admit, I have temporarily forgotten. We had a good band to accompany us and our principal, Thomas Gretzinger, would be on hand to give us leadership and support.

War was by far the main topic of our youthful conversations. We had opinions about which airplane was the best, which general or admiral most deserved medals, where the aircraft carriers were battling, who was the latest ace with the most kills, when President Roosevelt was next going to speak on the radio to the nation in one of his Fireside Chats.

I graduated in June of 1942, by which time we had been beaten back by the Japanese on all fronts. We never felt defeated and I had a not-so-secret hope that the war would last until I was old enough to join and get a few licks in myself. The bombing of Tokyo in April cheered us immensely. Our victories in the Battle of the Coral Sea in May and the Battle of Midway in June were all I could want for a graduation present.

Jule's wedding photo. August 1944.

My Sister Jule

This will be a short chapter because almost every other chapter mentions my sister in some way or the other. Jule was (as she still is) the greatest influence on my life. My parents were both ill from the time I was six and my three older brothers were just that, older. They had their own interests and those interests didn't always include me, or my sister for that matter. Being next to me in age gave Jule and me an extra bond that I never felt with anyone else in my family.

We played together when we were little. We pushed each other in my wagon, she helped me take care of my mongrel pup, Wimpy, and she was always there when I needed someone to share my joys or sorrows.

She is now a successful artist and always has half a dozen ideas ready to patent. She has a *joie de vivre* that women a third her age would be lucky to possess. She took care of our mother until her dying day and my father until he was put into a nursing home. She read my report cards and tried to make me come home at reasonable hours when my parents were too out of it to get involved.

We still see each other at least once a week and enjoy our past, present, and future together.

Courtesy Temple University Urban Archives

Pretzels

Can you believe that pretzels once cost a penny apiece? Now they have designer pretzels that cost as much as $1.25 each—that's without mustard. One finds them in all the malls, at sports events, and at busy intersections in Philadelphia, competing with the unwelcomed windshield washers for your time, money, peace of mind, and perhaps health. I think Philadelphia is properly the home of the big pretzel (little ones too).

Our pretzel man was always waiting for us at school. He was there with his pushcart at morning recess, lunchtime, and after school. While we were in school, he would pass the pretzels through the bars of the steel fence and we had to beg him for "more mustard please." After school we were allowed to spread as much mustard on our pretzel as we pleased. The spreader was a wooden paddle, something like a tongue depressor, only three times bigger.

I always searched for the pretzel with the most salt on it and licked half the salt off before I actually started to eat. That was somewhat hard to do because our pretzel man would never allow us to spread on more mustard once we chewed into his product.

You can always tell a person is from Philadelphia. I have never seen anyone not from Philadelphia spread mustard on pretzels. Even today, in a different city, people look askance when I ask for mustard to spread on even little pretzels out of a box. Those who know say, "Oh, you must be from Philadelphia."

I tried a dollar-and-a-quarter designer pretzel a few years ago in an upscale shopping mall. I couldn't even finish it. It was as bland as matzo crackers. The pretzel vendor had never heard of anyone spreading soft, runny mustard on a designer pretzel and looked at me as though I was an uncouth Neanderthal type. He must not have been from Philadelphia.

Now there are garlic or onion-flavored pretzels. Next there will be non-toxic, non-fattening, no-cholesterol, biodegradable, saffron-added, no-taste chunks of soggy dough they call pretzels. Please!

I'll try another designer pretzel when the next millennium arrives in five years. I hope by then they get back to where they were in the thirties.

The Knife Sharpener

Every few months the knife man would come around. He sharpened all sorts of cutting instruments from knives to scissors to axes to planing blades for carpenters. He usually had a bag full of knives and scissors for sale. I imagine he got them at auction or bought them from his customers. I don't think they were brand-new cutlery items and I don't think my mother ever bought anything from him.

My father always sharpened our knives by honing the knife against a wand-like sharpening tool whose horn handle matched that of the knives. If they were really dull he would use a whetstone. He would never use his leather honing strop for sharpening kitchen or tool shop instruments. That was reserved exclusively for his straightedge razor and perhaps once or twice for giving us a questionably deserved licking.

When the sharpening man came around with his treadle-operated grinder on his back he would shout out his particular sing-song announcement, "Scissssorrrs sharpened, kniiives sharpened." My mother would give us two or three pairs of scissors and I'd run out and stand in line with the other kids on our block with the same mission.

His stone must have been a foot in diameter, two inches thick, very smooth, and very, very heavy. The stand was like a modified four-legged high stool. The strap arrangement allowed him to carry the heavy machine around on his back like a knapsack.

The heavy wheel was connected to a leather belt and an eccentric gear attached to a foot treadle. Often he would take the scissors apart and sharpen each blade separately. With carpenter planing blades, he used a little jig to hold the blade steady as he moved it left and right across the face of the wheel while working the treadle with his foot. He had a cup of water into which he dunked the blade after each pass so that it wouldn't get too hot and cause the metal to lose its integrity.

He charged five cents to sharpen little paring knives and ten cents for big butcher knives and scissors. For the time and accuracy demanded for sharpening carpenters' planing blades he usually charged fifteen cents.

It seemed that every day we children were running errands for our parents and negotiating with adult businessmen who came down our alley. We handled change and had to be sure that the job was done right, the produce we bought was fresh, and there were twelve eggs to a dozen.

We learned to add and subtract in our heads, to shop, and to discriminate about the value or condition of what we were buying for our mothers. We had a great deal of responsibility. I won't make the age-old complaint that today's children aren't like we were when we were young. We had different problems and goals but I guess kids are always the same the world over no matter what century they are in.

My Brother John

John was the third child in our family of five. Next to my sister Jule, who was between us, John was the closest to me in both age and sentiment. Any sibling rivalry between my brothers and me was more pronounced with John. I guess that was because Ed and Dan were so much older than I and thus more removed from my own narrow sphere.

John picked on me sometimes and perhaps I bugged him too much sometimes. But he loved me and I loved him, and I spent more time with him than I did with Dan or Ed combined. He was killed in 1953 at the age of just thirty-three, leaving a wife and two kids, Jonathan, two years old, and Julia, two months old.

He had just begun his doctoral studies at the University of North Carolina and was planning to drive his old car over the mountains to a furniture factory to learn the practical aspects of furniture design. His friend persuaded him to go in his new car. Going around a mountain curve, his friend's car slipped off the roadway; in trying to get back on, the car flipped over. There were no seat belts in those days. John was thrown from the car and that was the end of my brother John.

John loved horses and then cars as he grew up. Several times a week during the summer months a man would come through our alley selling pony rides for ten cents. John saved his money and I don't think he ever missed a chance to ride. Often he'd pay for three or four rides on a long summer's evening. John could not have been older than nine at the time and I not more than five.

As the colder days of autumn approached the owner of the pony asked John if he'd like to take care of his steed during the winter. The owner was poor and couldn't afford to feed his pony for six months with no income. With surprisingly little objection from my father, the pact was agreed upon and within days a small pony stable appeared in one side of our double garage.

Before breakfast every morning and immediately after coming home from school, John would go to the garage and tend to the pony. Every day, rain or shine, sleet or snow, John would spend an hour or so riding around the neighborhood on his charge. Many times, after the sexton of the First Christian Science Church across the street went home, John would ride his pony on the church's winter lawn and let him eat the dried grass and shrubs.

In the beginning of this relationship between boy and pony the owner would come around every few days to check up on John and see how he was treating his most valuable asset. Soon convinced that John was loving and caring, the owner rarely visited. Finally, spring came and John had to give back his treasure. But from then on, whenever the man came around, he would let John ride for free, as soon as the paying customers were taken care of.

We had a wonderful photo of John riding his pony. The animal had reared high on his hind legs and John was waving his wide-brimmed ten-gallon hat in the sky just like John Wayne. Now we just have the picture of him with his mount.

John astride his steed around 1929.

At some point, long before he was an eligible driver at sixteen, John got an old Model T Ford. It was in remarkably good condition and I think he paid just thirty-five dollars for it. He worked on it with the same enthusiasm he gave the pony and soon it was in almost mint condition.

By carrying a week's movie advertisement on the back of his Model T, John got two free tickets to the Bala Theater. The Bala was a few cuts above the Hamilton or the Overbrook, as it showed foreign films and first-run Hollywood epics. The Ham and the OB have long since closed their doors, but the Bala is still in business showing quality films.

A lovely 1934 Ford wood station wagon followed the Model T with perhaps a few clunkers in between. Somehow, the front right window got a crack in it, and whenever anybody slammed the door, John would holler that the passenger had broken his window and would have to pay for it. I don't think the scam ever worked, and within days, everyone in the neighborhood was on to the trick.

The station wagon was for both business and pleasure; John used it to begin his egg business while still in his late teens and in high school. Many times, John took me with him on his wholesale egg purchasing trips to Lancaster County.

One Friday evening, we were in Paoli, heading west on the Lincoln Highway to an Amish farm to purchase eggs, when the headlights gave out. The police stopped us, and we had to sleep in the back of the wagon until daylight. I was no more than eleven and I loved the excitement of sleeping in the car while the traffic roared by all night long. I was never afraid because John was with me.

John had a natural talent for drawing and from my earliest recollection he was always drawing on scraps of paper and in notebooks. His imaginative comic characters could always be identified as friends or relatives or political figures. He poked fun at everyone and I know of no one who ever took offense at his jibes.

John's love for automobiles led him to design on paper and in clay model cars that are to this day ahead of their time in their lines and beauty. If any of his designs were still in existence, I'm sure Detroit would love to have them to work on. He also designed intricate logos and monograms. I still remember his JTH monogram which flowed together in one beautiful artistic expression.

My brother, John, in Italy. 1944.

Self portrait.

About six months before Pearl Harbor, John went to Puerto Rico to drive a bulldozer to help construct Borinquen Field, a huge new Army Air Corps base in the northwest corner of the island. My brother Ed had preceded him and I think helped him get the job. There, John indulged his childhood passion for horses and often rode full-sized horses during his time off.

Around March of 1942, he came home for a short visit, and in just a few weeks was grabbed up by the local draft board and sent to Camp Miles Standish on Cape Cod. In a few more months he was manning an antiaircraft battery in Liverpool to relieve British soldiers who were being sent to Africa to fight. He made friends in Liverpool and sent me the name of a girlfriend's little sister, with whom I corresponded for years. He had that job, manning an antiaircraft gun to protect Liverpool, until the Army learned that he was an experienced bulldozer operator.

One would think the Army would have made him a cook after learning he could run a bulldozer. Instead, they shipped him off to North Africa to help defeat Erwin Rommel. Within a week of landing in Africa he was on board a giant D-8 Caterpillar bulldozer for his Combat Engineers Battalion, this time for a lot less money.

He fought through North Africa, made the landings at Gela in Sicily on July 10, 1943, and at Salerno, Italy, on September 9. He had few days off and was in combat under enemy fire for more than 1,000 days. He still found time to send home V-Mail letters, and some of his exploits in Italy are in other chapters of this account.

About a month before the war ended in Europe, my cousin Ed Logue, a bombardier with the 95th Fighter Squadron of the 82nd

John the rower and me the passenger. 1929.

Fighter Group, managed to get a few days off from his combat flying in Italy to look up my brother John on March, 1945. The following letter was written to my brother Ed from Cousin Ed telling of their meeting:

Dear Ed:

Here is the letter the Hogans have been waiting for. I had a leave recently and in my wanderings went up to look for John.

I found him eating in the outfit's newly built mess hall. The chow was fair, the coffee poor, but I had some of both for I was starved. He was surprised, and laughed as did I, but we discovered that being in the mountains in Italy in the Army we still looked normal to each other. He still shaves once a week, or maybe that is an improvement. You Hogans were always backward and therefore fortunate in such matters. I was a bit heavier than when he last saw me in New Haven, some two and a half years ago. It took a while for us to get started talking. You find that the closer people are the longer it takes. But perhaps that seemed like hours and actually it was only a few minutes. He and I set about looking for his lieutenant climbing up and down among the pine trees. All picturesque we agreed but still a campsite. In due time we found them and they were gracious enough to give him a twenty-four hour pass. To tell you the truth it was more than either of us expected.

We set out for Florence and in due time arrived and strolled around the town. We found a Fifth Army leave restaurant but I wasn't welcome. (Ed was an officer and John was an enlisted man) The army doesn't recognize ties of blood and we had to eat separately. The difference between the gold bar and the stripes was inconveniencing but not insurmountable. John, by the way, doesn't wear his stripes. He says he often gets assigned to a job for another outfit and on occasion someone is likely to get annoyed and mutter, "if you had any stripes, I'd break you!" He still knows how to make the best of a bad time.

In Florence we got a comfortable room, beds with mattresses and sheets and in due time spent a talkative but comfortable night in them. There isn't much to do in one of these towns unless you are well acquainted with them so we just wandered about and finally rested our feet in a remote but sumptuous corner of the officer's club.

Back at the room we drank some American whiskey I had brought along and shot the breeze some more. We slept late the next day and wandered around some more. Ate. Splurged on a carriage ride about town. Looked in at the shops and the PX and a few other places and finally had to break it up and part, hoping we would see each other again sooner.

He did assure me that he has written you quite often and can't figure what the hell is the matter. (The letters you do get, does there seem to be anything wrong with them?) He seems a bit older, wiser, maturer and all that sort of thing but pretty much the same sort of guy. He liked England and had a good time there but hasn't particularly since. Although you are in a strange and new country, the chances are that being in the army you will only see a small part of it which will come to a deadly familiarity and dullness. His is now, I would say, a fairly dull life and at times he is at fault for not resigning himself to the army and relaxing but everyone can't do that. As a matter of fact he has serious doubts about me and my seeming complacency with this life. He needn't worry. I'm just resigned but I want to get out as much as he does. Anyway the pattern doesn't tend to make him informative. He is satisfied with the deal he has now weighing it against the only possible alternatives. Perhaps the biggest item that bothers him and the vast majority of ground force guys is that they have nothing definite to look forward to. He will have to sweat it out I guess.

That's about all. If you want anything, ask, go ahead. I'm looking forward to the day when all the Hogans and all the Logues can sit down and have a beer together with or without wives and other accouterments. I hear you're engaged my boy. Congratulations. Any pictures of the lion tamer. Will try to write Dan soon but you might make sure by sending him a copy of this.

All for now, Ed

With more discharge points than needed, John was home and free by November 1945. Our family had started an agricultural limestone business in New Hope, Pennsylvania, by then. He joined in until we went bust. He spent too much time in the Valley Forge Army Hospital, just a few hundred yards from where I now live, combating his war-incurred ulcers. Then he was involved in his own small upholstery business. Finally he found himself, and matriculated at the University of Chicago where he obtained a Bachelor of Fine Arts degree, a wife, and two great kids. A month in North Carolina, and it was all over.

His son Jonathan is a wonderful actor and his daughter Julia is a great mother of four. His wife lives in Maine and I still miss him.

Making Ice Cream

We didn't have thirty-one flavors of ice cream in the thirties. We didn't even have twenty-eight. But what we had was twice as good as Ben and Jerry's. Perhaps it was because we made our own ice cream and didn't get it from the frozen food section of the supermarket. Come to think of it, I don't even remember our A&P having a frozen food section.

Anyway, our Abbott's milk came unhomogenized—meaning that every bottle of milk had at least four inches of rich, thick cream floating on top. When the family was really flush we got as much as two quarts of milk a day for us five children and two adults. We never heard of two-percent milk or skim milk. During the summer, and even sometimes in the winter, my mother would pour off the cream top and save it for our Saturday afternoon ice cream making session. Around four o'clock on Saturday, we would get out the big one-gallon wooden ice cream bucket and set it on the back steps. My mother would mix the cream with cut up strawberries or peaches and pour in a little vanilla extract for that special flavor she knew we loved.

We cut a big chunk of ice off the fifty-pound block in our icebox, wrapped it in a towel, and broke it into pieces small enough to put around the metal mixer that was positioned in the center of the wooden bucket. With each layer of ice we poured rock salt to help the ice melt faster and thus draw the heat from the metal can of cream.

That trick of using ice to suck out heat stood me in good stead when I was on maneuvers with the 11th Airborne Division during a beastly hot North Carolina summer in 1951. Then, I showed my buddies how to cool a six-pack of beer cans by slowly dripping a gallon of gasoline we siphoned from our Jeep over the closely stacked cans. The quick evaporation of the gasoline, as it dripped on the beer cans, would cool our drinks to 40 degrees in just a few minutes at a cost of just one gallon of gas. I hope the taxpayers will forgive me for squandering ten cents' worth of gas forty years ago. That was the best beer I ever tasted!

Back to the thirties. We all volunteered to turn the crank on the ice cream maker because then we got to lick the paddles when the job was done. We were eager to finish the job and too often opened the can before the mix had hardened. But once the crank became really hard to turn we knew the treat was ready.

We all got full dishes of ice cream, and often we had chocolate syrup or homemade strawberry jam to pour over the dessert. We had to finish the whole gallon at one sitting because the ice cream would just melt in an old-fashioned icebox.

On a few occasions, we actually bought hand-packed Breyers Ice Cream at Bergman's drug store at the bottom of the hill on which we lived. That was an even more special treat because we would always get some exotic flavor such as butter pecan or burnt almond. But looking back, absolutely nothing compared to the ice cream we made on our back steps.

The Tustin Playground

During the first half of the thirties, there was a large empty lot just a block away from our house at 61st and Columbia. The lot was huge, bordered by 60th Street and Columbia and Lancaster Avenues. It was just across the street from Overbrook High School, my family's and Wilt Chamberlain's alma mater. The lot had hills and valleys and offered us an opportunity to do almost anything we wanted. Nobody bothered us. It was kept clean and no one thought of dumping trash or parking shopping carts there. Adults used it for cookouts and picnics. Teenagers and men used it for whatever sport was in season, baseball, football, and even basketball played on a dirt floor.

We kids dug tunnels into the sides of the hills, built forts, and made fire pits for cooking meals. Before the days of aluminum foil, my father taught us how to gut a chicken and wrap it in a layer of mud. The same with potatoes. We would dig a small hole in the ground about six inches deep and a foot across. We'd then light a fire and when the coals were bright and hot we'd drop the mud-encased chicken into the middle of the newly made charcoal. After a while, we'd drop the potatoes into the embers beside the chicken. Or perhaps it was the other way around. Which came first, the chicken or the potato? I forget which takes longer to cook. When we peeled the mud off the chicken, the feathers came off as well.

Anyway, with a knife and a saltshaker, there was nothing that tasted half as good. Colonel Sanders would have starved had he started his business anywhere within range of our "Finger Lickin' Good" chicken. Of course we cooked hot dogs and toasted rolls and corn in the husks on our campfires as well. But nothing beat our chicken.

The hills on our delightful undeveloped playground were short but steep and in the winter we would sled down them on our Flexible Flyers. In the summer, we would sled down the hills in big cardboard boxes. More often than not we would upset the box halfway down and tumble the rest of the way head over heels. We careened down the hills on bikes, wagons, and anything with wheels and some things without wheels.

Doomsday was not far off. One summer day, some engineers and architects accompanied by a few politicians paid our preserve a visit. I was unaware of the catastrophe that awaited us, but noticed an uneasy feeling among the adults who were using the site after they talked with the enemy aliens from city hall.

Sure enough, our empty lot was to be developed into an official playground by the Philadelphia Department of Recreation to honor someone named Ernest Tustin. To this day I never knew who he was or why they would dishonor his name by destroying our recreation site. We didn't need urban renewal nor did we want it. We liked things just the way they were.

Soon, barricades went up and construction vehicles moved in. Most of the vehicles were horse powered, including horse drawn scoops that worked like frontend loaders as they scooped out dirt and leveled our wonderful hills and filled our enchanting valleys. Next came the fence to keep people out. It was a high iron bar type with spikes at the top and big brick columns every fifteen or twenty feet. A big iron gate was put at the formerly free entrance.

Next came the cinders.

My, how they brought in truckload after truckload of dirty, sharp cinders for our playground surface. They buried the entire playground under at least a foot of the filthy stuff. It wasn't until years later that I learned that the cinder supply contract had been a payoff for a politician trying to get rid of his cinders and bilk the city and us children as well. We all had cinders embedded in our knees and hands until our mothers declared the new playground off limits.

They built a sort of half-baked gym that closed almost as soon as it was dedicated and opened to the public, never to open again. My neighbors stayed away in droves. We children couldn't dig in cinders, create a tunnel, sled or slide down nonexistent hills or, God forbid, light a fire on city property.

About a decade after the city destroyed our playground by building their playground, the cinders were removed and the good old-fashioned dirt was replaced. By that time, I was too old or maybe too disgusted to enjoy it. I still drive by the Tustin Playground every few years and wonder why it all happened the way it did. "If it ain't broke, don't fix it."

On a recent inspection tour of Tustin, I found it in rather poor shape with sections of the spiked fence and brick columns destroyed. But there was one beautiful ray of hope for old Mr. Tustin. The City of Philadelphia had installed a large, clean, well-managed swimming pool. When I last visited the playground, the pool was full of happy adults and children swimming and cooling themselves on a hot August afternoon.

The new swimming pool at the Tustin playground.

Century-old Philadelphia horse troughs saved from the wreckers sledge hammers.

Horse Troughs

Horses were very important to our daily life while I was growing up in the thirties. They pulled ice wagons, milk wagons, junk wagons, trash wagons, and even a form of bulldozer that my father used when excavating basements for the houses he built.

Horses need feed and water. Carrying feed was an easy matter for the driver. A simple canvas bucket strapped under the nose of a horse would sustain him during the day.

Water was a different matter. The driver could not easily carry a sufficient amount of water to see the horse through a long hot summer day. Enter the WSPCA (Women's Society for the Prevention of Cruelty to Animals) and the WCTU (Women's Christian Temperance Union). As the nineteenth century closed, these two benevolent groups worked to put in place hundreds of beautifully carved granite horse troughs. There wasn't a major intersection or crossroads in Philadelphia that wasn't graced with these working works of water art.

The WCTU naturally was promoting water as an alternative to alcohol, and what more positive way than to install water fountains and troughs around the city to slake the thirst of hard-working people and horses. The WSPCA was interested in the welfare of all animals. They even saw to it that the overflow from the fountains spilled into water trays for dogs.

As a child I spent many happy hours on a hot summer's day splashing in the fresh, cool water in the granite horse tough at 63rd and Lancaster, just opposite the firehouse my grandfather had built.

Forty years went by with little thought to horse troughs until I happened upon a horse trough destruction party at K&A (Kensington and Allegheny). The Philadelphia Street Department crew was going at the beautiful round trough with sledge hammers. It seems that over recent years more than fifty cars had self-destructed on the black and white painted striped sculpture. I was towing my tilt-top trailer behind my pickup. I offered the crew thirty-five dollars to take a long lunch and told them that their problem would be solved before they finished their hoagies. The demolition crew was most amenable to my proposal, and as soon as they left, I tilted my trailer, jacked up the one-ton water trough, and used my "come-along" to drag it onto my trailer. True to my word, I was gone before their lunch was over. The trough now graces my patio and every day I thank Annie L. Lowery for her donation of it a hundred years ago.

Over the years I have saved about ten horse troughs from destruction. One I traded to the artist Ben Shahn for some sketches, and it now is in his yard in Roosevelt, New Jersey, where his widow Bernarda still enjoys it. Another is safely in place at the Old Second Street Market in the refurbished Society Hill section of Philadelphia. Others are around my home. But the important thing is that finally someone in City Hall got the message, and horse troughs are no longer destroyed as a convenience to cars. Slowly, one by one, they are being resurrected and placed in public places around the city to begin a second century of beauty and practicality.

Root Beer Making

Pepsi's Jingle:

Pepsi Cola hits the spot,
Twelve full ounces,
That's a lot,
Twice as much for a nickel too,
Pepsi Cola's the drink for you.

Our Version:

Pepsi Cola is a rotten drink,
Toss it down the kitchen sink,
Tastes like vinegar
Looks like ink,
Pepsi Cola is a rotten drink.

We couldn't afford a nickel for Pepsi or Coke in the mid-thirties, we could afford a penny to make our own root beer. Then and now, I am sure it was better than the two name brands. It was also a heck of a lot of fun concocting the mixture.

We started out with two small bottles of Hires Root Beer Extract, three small cakes of Fleischmann's Yeast, about five pounds of sugar, six gallons of water, lots of bottles, caps, and a bottle capper. We used a large ten-gallon porcelain pot to mix everything together. We always had a hundred or more empty bottles on hand and it was my job to wash them thoroughly in the basement laundry tub. We usually began the root beer process early on a Saturday morning in late spring, just before school let out for the long hot summer. Into five or six gallons of water we dumped the root beer extract, then crumbled in the yeast. We stirred it just a little, enough to mix the ingredients well, but not enough to cause the mixture to bubble over. We heated the mixture and then added the sugar to help the yeast along.

Within just an hour or two, the root beer was ready to bottle. We had the bottles ready on one side, the caps and capper on the other, and the tub in the middle. We usually worked at the bottom of the cellar stairs next to the back cellar door.

I don't remember which job fell to which of my siblings. I was too young to ladle the mixture from the tub into a funnel placed in each bottle. Sometimes I was allowed to push the lever down on the capper to secure the cap around the neck of each bottle. I don't think any two bottles were the same. We even had some full and half-gallon jugs with screw-on caps that we filled. They would be saved for when we had a party or when we were sure we would drink a whole gallon at one sitting. After filling all the bottles and rinsing off the sticky residue, we stacked the bottles in a small closet under the stairs.

Then we waited and we waited and we waited.

Finally, in the middle of the night or on a hot afternoon, we knew the root beer was ready because we usually heard an exploding bottle nearly knock the door off the closet. We ran down the stairs to the basement, fetched a few bottles off the shelf, washed them off in the laundry tub, and carried them triumphantly upstairs to the kitchen.

We raided the icebox, chipped some ice off the big hundred-pound block, and filled our glasses. To this day I have never tasted anything so good.

A few weeks ago I went to half a dozen stores trying to buy Hires Root Beer Extract. No one had any. When I called the home office in Stratford, Connecticut, the public relations person told me they had stopped making it just recently due to poor sales. Ah me!

The Greatest Tree House
in the Whole Wide World

My willow tree house was the greatest tree house in the whole wide world. It was a multi-storied affair and had several means of access and egress. You could climb a ladder made from sticks nailed cross-ways to the trunk, you could shinny up the fireman's escape pole, or you could use my private elevator made from a double set of block and tackle. You merely had to sit on the bos'n's chair and pull yourself up. As the pulley had a four-to-one advantage and I weighed less than one hundred pounds, I needed to exert just twenty-five pounds of pull. I wonder if they teach that concept in new math?

An even more exotic way to get to my tree house was to jump from the nearby roof of our breakfast room or to swing Tarzan-fashion from my satellite tree house about twenty-five feet away. Tarzan was my hero in those days and I never missed a movie about his adventures as King of the Jungle. In features or perilous serials he faced certain death each week, always wiggling out of it in the next installment the following Saturday at the Hamilton Theater matinee.

I aped (if you'll pardon the pun) his every movement and copied most of the things he had installed in his tree house with Jane. I was never able to duplicate the fan he had placed over his dining room table high in a baobab tree. Of course I really didn't need a fan. Nor did I

Our children, step-children and neighborhood kids in our tree house. Notice the elevator on a spool.

have a pet like Cheetah, his little ape, to turn the crank that operated the fan.

Anyway, after a year or so, I built a roof on my tree house to keep out the rain and side walls to keep out the cold. I then built a smaller tree house in another willow about twenty-five feet across the concrete driveway. I wanted private access to that tree house as too many visitors came to my high-rise abode to distract me from whatever business I was engaged in at the time.

For the longest time I couldn't figure out how Tarzan was able to swing so easily from tree to tree and fly over miles and miles of jungle in such a short time. It finally dawned on me that there must have been a whole crew of natives down on the ground whose only job was to position swinging vines so Tarzan could swing from one tree to the next without ever touching the ground.

If he could do it so could I. I didn't have a whole crew of natives so I had to reposition my own vine each time I made a Tarzan-like swing. I would climb down after each aerial flight to reposition the second rope that led to my satellite tree house. Then, when I leaped from my first tree house and swung out to the apogee of my first rope,

Tarzan movie poster.

the second rope would be in exactly the right place for the mid-air transfer and allow me to continue my flight to my retreat. After I perfected the maneuver with the first few swings I kept the second vine in place so that I could impress my friends when they happened by.

I don't think my mother noticed that the aerial transfer occurred over the concrete driveway, or she would have made me cease and desist forthwith.

In the summer, I spent more than one night in my tree house. I watched the stars as my home rocked gently in the wind. In the winter I would haul up buckets of snowballs and rain them down on family, friend, and foe alike. In the spring and fall I would sit in my aerie and read Big Little Books or just look out the windows at the passing scene. Then I would curl up and go to sleep.

Perhaps my childhood tree house was only the *second* best in the whole world. As an adult I worked with my own children to build a tree house equipped with a stove as well as an elevator. We had oil lamps and sometimes electricity, with the help of a small generator. The main tree house was connected by cable car to another tree 200 feet away.

Today one has to have a building permit to build a tree house and seven different inspectors come around to harass you. My friend, Richard Holland, an architect in El Cerrito, California, built a nifty tree house a few years ago. It had stained glass windows and beautiful carved staircases to go from one floor to the next. It even had a few skylights.

The town fathers soon issued a condemnation and ordered the tree house torn down as it violated sixteen or more building codes. It had no concrete foundation. It had no plumbing. The wiring hadn't been inspected, despite the fact that there was no electricity in the first place. On and on ad nauseam ad infinitum.

Richard put a sign in his front yard calling it an environmental sculpture with a price tag of $25,000. He never sold his work of art, and it wasn't torn down. The last I heard the zoning commission was busy rewriting the law.

Snow

I never checked with the weather bureau, but I truly believe that we had more snow when I was growing up than we do now, with the possible exception of the winter of 1994.

We never had snow days off from school. We walked the six blocks in rain, hail, sleet, or snow but not in the dark of night like the postman is supposed to do.

I always had an igloo in the backyard from the first to last snowfall of the season. To keep it frozen, I would spray it with water before going in for dinner, and after a few sprays, my igloo became as solid as a fort. We ate in the igloo and drank hot chocolate and had a great time playing Eskimo-house.

We built forts and had pitched battles with the kids next door. We built shelves into the inside walls to hold both provisions and ammunition. I cut out windows for light and a hole in the roof for smoke to exit. Old blankets provided a dry and comparatively warm floor to sit on. I spent many happy hours in my snow domes. On a few occasions, I made a two-story igloo by using a sheet of old plywood for the second-floor deck. But that was a lot of work.

My igloo-building abilities stood me in good stead for the winter of 1952. I built and lived in an igloo for six weeks while on maneuvers at Fort Drum in the northern snowbelt of New York. I had one of the best and most comfortable igloos in the whole 11th Airborne Division.

To my knowledge it was the only igloo in my regiment that had an indoor fireplace. For the entire six weeks, I don't think the temperature ever got above freezing. My platoon leader, Ken Marden, seemed to find several excuses a day to come and visit me and discuss important matters concerning my job.

From my earliest recollection, I had a Flexible Flyer sled that saw a lot of action. I also had cheap skis at a very early age. We used to sled down the steep hill by the Pennsylvania Railroad tracks at 62nd and Lancaster Avenue in big cardboard boxes. There was a sort of ski jump halfway down the hill and we would often careen into space, upsetting and spilling out of our boxes. I guess that's why I like Calvin and Hobbes so much. That comic strip pair is always flying into space from impossibly steep mountains.

My favorite snow sport when I was around ten years old was "bumpering." We rarely had snow plows clear our streets and the city never salted the roads. We would wait at a stop sign or a red light at a snow-covered intersection for a car. Cars had bumpers that weren't recessed into the rear end, and we could grab onto them with ease. We would get down on our haunches and hold on while the driver sped off. If he saw us he would sometimes try to shake us off by going over bare spots or hot manhole covers. We would hang on for blocks, four or five of us hanging on for dear life.

Some of the more accomplished bumper experts could actually let go of one bumper of a car that was going in a direction they didn't want to go, and, while still skidding across the snow on just their shoes, would grab another bumper going the right way. I don't think I ever did that. It was too crazy for me. I don't ever remember anyone getting hurt doing such a trick. But we made sure we never did it near home for fear our mothers or siblings would see us and blow the whistle.

Of course we also "bumpered" using sleds and would be able to pull ourselves ahead of the car towing us by a sort of "crack the whip" motion. That would scare the drivers which was an added thrill for us. I never told my children the "bumper" tale, and I hope my grandson doesn't read this.

Mother, Dad, Dan, Jule, John, Ed, and me.

On the front steps at Cape May. Top to bottom: Gordon, Uncle Ed, Frank, Ellen, John with the boat, and Ed.

The Logues:
My Cousins, Uncle Ed and Aunt Rene

I can barely remember my Uncle Ed Logue, who died when I was just six years old. In addition to owning a large three-story summer home in Cape May, Uncle Ed headed a large household at 2020 Mount Vernon Street in the swank Fairmount section of Philadelphia. The town house was just eight blocks from City Hall. The neighborhood fell onto hard times in the fifties and became pretty much a slum. Now gentrification has refurbished the area, and it is again a sought-after, upscale place to live.

2020 was a house with a very small back yard. A fascinating double Dutch–French door led from the living room onto a tiny side yard. The lower part opened like a regular double Dutch door, and the upper part had conventional windows that slid up high enough so an adult could walk through the door to the outside. I loved the complicated way the combination door and window opened and shut. For me the best part of 2020 was the long banister from the third to first floor down which I slid a thousand (well, maybe a dozen) times.

The top-floor front room was the bedroom for all four boys: Ed, Gordon, John, and Frank, each a year apart in age. Ellen, two years younger than Frank, had her own bedroom on the third floor. The third floor middle also had a room for the live-in maid and cook, first Jennie and then Winnie, both Irish immigrants. The large well-lit back room was for play. I couldn't participate, but I remember watching my older cousins melt lead and pour the hot liquid metal into soldier molds. A dozen different government agencies must outlaw that kind of play today. The playroom also had hundreds of wooden building blocks of every shape imaginable. My Aunt Rene had been a kindergarten teacher and had a thousand ways to entertain small children with toys and games.

For several Thanksgivings, I was taken to the Logues as a prelude to watching the annual Gimbel Brothers parade. The parade route went up 21st Street, just a half-block from 2020. This meant that on cold Thanksgiving mornings we could run back to 2020 for hot cocoa and then go back to watching the clowns, the bands, and, the biggest treat of all, Santa Claus riding by on a huge float. In that pre-television era the parade was a much more impressive and well-attended event than it is now. Watching a parade in person is a million times better than watching it on TV.

During the Depression the Logues lived on the $132 a month from their late father's insurance policy in a house provided by the generosity of our Uncle Ed Fay, brother of the Logue's and our mothers. 2045 North 62nd Street was one-half of a semi-detached house in the Overbrook section of West Philadelphia, just three blocks from our home on Columbia Avenue. The children, ranging from seven to fourteen, were yanked out of the prestigious Notre Dame Academy on Rittenhouse Square and transferred to public schools near their new home. At NDA they had a teacher for every ten classmates; now there was one teacher for every thirty or forty!

One good thing about their moving to Overbrook was that almost every day we Hogans saw a lot more of the Logues. My sister Jule somehow invaded the boys' sport of roller skate hockey on 62nd Street and often played their rough and tumble game. Some of us were even in the same classes at school. Now Thanksgivings were spent at our house with all ten children, Aunt Rene, and my parents gathered around the dining room table. It took three or four extra leaves in the table to accommodate us all.

Like the Hogans, the Logues converted their third floor into an income-producing apartment. And like our family, the Logues, while having friends visit, were sometimes embarrassed when the renters, having no separate entrance, would walk right in as though they belonged there. Though we installed electric refrigerators in our apartments to attract tenants, neither family had electric refrigerators at the time. They were too expensive, so we used ice. My cousin John recently told me that once, when his mother thought the tenants were out, she asked him to go up to the third floor and get some ice cubes for a summer lemonade. As it turned out the lady tenant was home. The tenant caught John raiding the refrigerator and severely chastised him. We rarely explained our dire straits to our friends and left them to wonder who the people were that walked into our houses.

◆ Ed ◆

Ed was the oldest of the five. Like my brother Dan, he was so much older than I that I had little to do with him. My most poignant memory of Ed was on the day my mother was buried in November, 1941. I had attended the funeral Mass, but Dad thought I should not see the interment. Ed was designated to drive me home and stay with me until the burial was over and the family came back from the cemetery. A similar thing happened in 1953 after the funeral of my brother John. Following interment, which I watched, I again found myself in the same car with Ed, who drove me home from Camp Hill, Pennsylvania.

Ed Logue went to Yale and graduated in 1942. After organizing the Yale dining hall and maintenance workers union, he joined the Army Air Corps and became a bombardier flying out of Italy. He participated in several raids on Germany and ended the war without a scratch. He was one of few volunteers to be selected as bombardiers on P-38 fighter planes. The Air Force sought to develop extremely accurate bombing techniques. Most people scoff when I tell them about those unusual P-38 fighter bombers. The Air Force was trying to develop small, high speed strategic bombers to take out dams and other top priority targets, and cousin Ed was selected for the initial tests.

After the war Ed sped through Yale Law School and worked briefly as a labor lawyer. In 1948 he joined Connecticut's newly elected governor, Chester Bowles, as his legal assistant. When President Truman named Bowles ambassador to India, Ed, with his new wife Margaret, went along with the Ambassador, again as his legal assistant. In the decades to follow Ed served some seven years as New Haven's Development Administrator and a similar number of years as Chief Executive Officer of the New York (State) Urban Development Corporation with a multi-billion dollar budget. Ed also served six years as Director of the Boston Redevelopment Authority. He is now a consultant and lives on Martha's Vineyard.

◆ Gordon ◆

Next was Cousin Gordon, another Yale College and Yale Law School graduate. As an adolescent, I remember Gordon's extraordinary talent for winning card games. He improved that skill all through his life. One Friday evening when I was about ten, the older boys were playing poker in our breakfast room. I whined to get in on the action. Finally they let me play. Gordon took my entire fifteen cents in about five minutes. I couldn't believe it! As I looked aghast at my empty pot, he gave me back the money and admonished me to learn more about the game before I risked my fortune. I still gamble a bit, but I am very, very careful.

In the years that followed Gordon was a real bread winner. He died in the summer of 1988, shortly after ending his business career as Secretary, General Counsel, and Senior Vice President of the Pennwalt Corporation, a Fortune 500 multinational company.

During World War II, Gordon was a navigator on a B-24 Liberator Bomber and, like his brother Ed, flew out of Italy. While in training in the South I remember reading his letters about how he was awed by the brilliant stars in their galaxies as he charted his plane's position in the clear night skies over Texas. He flew but one combat bombing mission over Germany before the war ended. He won so much money playing cards in the Air Force that he helped supplement his and his brother Frank's GI Bill of Rights stipend through Yale. In December of 1952, a few weeks after I got out of the Army, Gordon asked me to be his best man when he married Susan Lancaster in Lincoln, Nebraska. I was honored, and while there met my future wife, Olenka Stepanek.

Gordon was generous to a fault. He and Sue, along with their children Jim and Emily, hosted family Thanksgiving dinners in their Merion, Pennsylvania, home for thirty years. He once bought a piece of a boxer. Unless my memory fails me, the fighter was more used to lying on the canvas than winning bouts. Gordon and Sue's second home on Martha's Vineyard was open to everyone. He had a special love for the island and is now buried there. He was his mother's main moral and financial support until she died.

◆ John ◆

Next was Cousin John, the academician of both families. In some ways I suppose I am closer to him than his siblings because he has lived in nearby Swarthmore for the past forty years. He has a Bachelor of Arts degree from Central High School in Philadelphia. I believe Central High is the only high school in the country allowed to bestow BAs on their graduates. After being drafted, he scored 154 in his Army tests and joined the select 10th Mountain Infantry Division in 1943, one of the few combat units that required five references to join. He underwent a year of arduous skiing and mountain climbing training at Camp Hale, Colorado. For health reasons, he was transferred out just before the unit went to fight in Italy. John ended up the war as an archivist at the Command and General Staff School at Fort Leavenworth, Kansas, where he helped catalog all of the reports on the battles the Army fought throughout the war.

He still sees his old comrades and is proud of the fact that of his old 10th Mountain Division, which includes Senator Bob Dole, has the highest proportion of active members, more than any other unit in the country. It is said that interest in and respect for 10th Mountain Division veterans' skiing helped fuel the modern billion dollar ski industry in the United States.

John is a hopeless punster. It is sometimes hard to get out three uninterrupted sentences without John making a pun of something you have just said. I was fortunate to have John's invaluable assistance in proofreading these childhood accounts.

Last winter I went skiing with John and his seventy-year-old ski buddy veterans. It was inspiring to ski with this wonderful group of men and listen to them recall their half-century-old exploits of heroism and friendship. After a hard day's skiing we had a memorial service for their departed comrades. John follows the adventures of the 10th with patriotic devotion. As of this writing, the 10th Mountain is deployed on peacekeeping missions in Somalia and Haiti. John is a Senior Vice President of the United World Federalist Association and is presently putting the finishing touches on his latest book, entitled *Strengthening the United Nations.*

◆ Frank ◆

Frank, the youngest boy, was the boy closest in age to me, and before the war we went on many forays together. We sledded and skated together and sometimes sneaked into movies with other kids in the neighborhood and into swimming pools at night. Frank went to the University of North Carolina for a year, transferred to Yale, and, after one semester, enlisted in the Air Corps. Frank was in the Army Special Training Program at the University of Iowa when the Battle of the Bulge was fought. He was yanked out of college and rushed to France. There he finished the war as a Combat Infantryman with a severe case of trench foot due to cold and wet combat conditions.

After the war he returned to Yale College and Yale Law School. He became a lawyer and mayor of New Haven, Connecticut for two terms in the 1970s. Frank's 15 minutes (actually about twelve hours) of fame was when Queen Elizabeth and Prince Philip visited Yale to help celebrate the Bicentennial in 1976. As mayor it was his duty, along with the governor, to greet the queen and prince. Frank rode with the prince in a motorcade through downtown New Haven. On behalf of the City of New Haven he gave Her Majesty a silver tray and Prince Philip a made-in-New Haven Winchester hunting rifle. Frank once told me that while he was preparing for the royal visit one of his thousands of Irish constituents came up to him and said, "Surely, Frank, you are not going to welcome that British b--?" Frank replied, "It's my job Mac. Somebody has to do it." Since Gordon died, Frank hosts the family Thanksgiving dinners in New Haven with his wife Mary Ann, an Episcopal priest.

◆   Ellen   ◆

Cousin Ellen, for the longest time nicknamed "Babe," is a retired teacher who lives in Berkeley and now represents retired members on the Board of Directors of the National Education Association (NEA). She flies all over the country on NEA-related business. Like me, she was the youngest of five children. We had a particular bond in that respect, even though she was a girl. I remember playing Monopoly with her, Frank, and my sister Jule on rainy afternoons and building sand castles on the beach at Cape May. She was only seven when her father died.

Ellen is probably the only one in the two families who was sure from earliest childhood where she would go to college. My Uncle Ed Logue's sister, Sister Maria Kostka, founded Chestnut Hill College in Philadelphia and was its first president. Ellen followed in her aunt's footsteps and graduated from Chestnut Hill College. She later received a master's degree from Catholic University in Washington, D.C. After working a short time for the Philadelphia Housing Authority, she packed her bags and headed west to teach at the college level and then the elementary school level in Berkeley. Ellen comes east several times a year. I still don't see enough of her.

Our last Hogan-Logue-Fay family reunion was in 1984. Since then my Cousin Gordon and my brother Dan have died. There are four Logues and three Hogans left from our generation, and we aren't getting any younger.

The fountain today.

Our backyard in the 30s with the fountain.

6044 Columbia Avenue

A few years ago my brother Ed and I stopped by our old home in West Philadelphia. We stood for a while by the side gate and reminisced. The new owner, Mr. Riley, asked if he could help us. When I told him we were born in his house, at first he didn't believe us.

I began to describe the large round pillar in the basement on which my father had painted a mural, the sliding doors in the second-floor bathroom and the master bedroom and the window over the second-floor bathroom that I used to crawl out of on my alternate way to the roof.

He said, "Well, I guess you were born here; would you like to come in and look around?" We jumped at the opportunity and Mr. Riley was a bit astonished as we foretold what we would see before we entered a room, hall, or stairway.

6044 was a well-built house, made of brick with a stone foundation. My father took exceptional care and pride in building it because it was to be the final home he would build for his family and we all expected to live in it a lot longer than we did.

My father was always building something, improving things, working on an elaborate garden complete with a fountain and fish pond. The small pond was inlaid with mosaic tile and water spurted from the mouth of a face set into the wall.

All that's left of the fountain now is the face. When I was a baby, there was an open porch over the first floor porch. Soon after I was born, my father built a large study over the porch with an entrance from the master bedroom. When one of us became ill, my mother would put us in there next to her bedroom. I still remember an exotic little spirit lamp that she placed by my bed. She put some sort of medicine in a small cup and the heat from the lamp sent sweet medicinal smells wafting through the room and made me feel warm and loved.

Long before I was born, we had a back porch that my father had converted into an enclosed breakfast room. He waterproofed the walls of our two-car garage so we could fill it with water and swim and sail boats. We had an elf or two on the lawn and flowers everywhere.

The biggest holiday I remember besides Christmas was Flag Day. Every June 14, our house was festooned with dozens of flags, buntings, and banners. There must have been some sort of undeclared contest on our block to see whose household was the most patriotic. We decorated our bikes and trikes by weaving red, white, and blue paper streamers in the spokes. We wore Uncle Sam hats and red, white, and blue sashes across our chests. Today, one rarely sees more than just a

Ed, John and Dan celebrate Flag Day. Around 1924.

lonely flag flying in a front yard on the Fourth of July. I haven't seen any houses decorated with flags on Flag Day for forty years or more.

In the mid-thirties, when we were at our financial and, I guess, psychological nadir as a family, my father converted our third floor into an apartment to earn extra money. The front room had been Dan and Ed's bedroom. The rear was for the maids and there was a store room in the middle. Dan was away at Yale, we had no maids, and Ed was moved down to the second floor.

My father created a kitchen out of the store room by installing a gas stove and refrigerator as well as a kitchen sink. I remember helping him hang new wallpaper and the long trestle table he used to lay out the wallpaper rolls. The paste brush must have been a foot wide and it was fun helping him. He installed a door and a lock at the bottom of the stairs for privacy.

Our first tenants were the Frazers. She was a medical doctor and he was a drinker. They had a big gray schnauzer and several times a day would march through our living room on their trips up and down to their apartment. We got thirty-five dollars a month rent and it was a great help, but my father got into some sort of argument with the Frazers over their dog or the way they parked their car, blocking our driveway. Anyway, they were gone one day.

Our next tenants were the Vargas. Jackie and Charley were so nice to my sister and me. Charley, the son of the former Hungarian Consul General in Montreal, was a college graduate and pumped gas at the Atlantic station at 62nd and Lancaster. I know Jackie had some sort of job but I can't remember what it was. My sister Jule stayed friends with them for thirty or forty years after they left.

Lots of horses and wagons and motor trucks passed through our alley every day, but it wasn't a block-long junk yard. There was one trucking operation in particular that I loved to watch: the city trash wagons pulled by horses. The trash wagons were big square dumpster-like steel boxes about eight-by-eight feet square and six feet deep. They were set in a steel frame fitted with four solid rubber-tired wheels and a driver's seat. The horse would pull the empty wagon down the alley, while two men heaved the ashes and what little trash we had into the box.

Right across 61st Street was the collection point of the wagons. When they were full, each wagon would pull up beside a long tractor trailer. A crane truck would lift empty boxes off the trailer and set them aside for a moment. Then the crane would lift the full box from the horse-drawn cart and place it on the trailer. When the trailer was loaded with full boxes and the horse carts with empty ones, the trailer would be taken to the dump to be unloaded. Meanwhile the horse-drawn carts would begin filling up again.

The horses would start and stop at a whistle from the trash men. A spokesman for the Philadelphia Streets Department recently told me that this system was the most efficient, cost effective, and ecologically sound method ever used in the city. Alas, they now use $100,000 diesel compactors, and the trucks won't start and stop with a whistle.

After my mother died, I was sent away to boarding school. My brother Dan, by then a naval officer, paid my tuition. When I came home for Christmas vacation in 1942, we didn't live there anymore. My father had sold everything we had and we had moved to a small apartment. I have just two things from our old house, a beautiful miniature painting of a roadside shrine in Italy that my father painted, and a needlepoint that my mother's mother made when she was just twelve years old. The work was of Christ's head and crown of thorns. It won first prize in my grandmother's class at the Centennial Exhibition held in Philadelphia in 1876.

My father painted this tiny wayside chapel while in Italy in 1925.
Notice St. Peter's in the background.

Mr. Riley is in the towing business and he knocked down the back garden wall. Where we once had trees and play equipment and tents and nets and a pretty garden with flowers and vegetables, the yard is now filled with tow trucks and assorted automobile parts.

Several of the houses on our block are now in a sad state of repair, but some are still in excellent condition. I wonder which way the block will go, toward gentrification or a slum. The huge back alley in which we played roller skate hockey on the smooth concrete seems to have shrunk into a long, narrow, potholed parking lot for all sorts of dilapidated cars and countless trash cans, some empty and some half filled with their guts spilled out over the potholes.

The Japanese yew trees my father planted seventy years ago are now giants over thirty feet tall. The grass is green and high and needs a good mowing and the hedges are left to spread over the sidewalks inhibiting passage. They look as if they haven't been trimmed since I last did the job in the summer of 1942, the year we lost the house to the bank.

Half of the sycamore trees my father planted on both sides of the 6000 block of Columbia Avenue are gone with apparently no thought of ever replacing them with new ones. I guess since people now move every two or three years they see no point in spending money on planting trees for someone else to enjoy. Maybe they don't realize that a tree out front increases the value of a house. But what do I know? I like trees, have planted over a thousand, and feel a sense of loss looking at a half-barren Columbia Avenue.

My favorite room in our old house was the third floor back. I loved to climb out the window and jump over the four-foot void to the roof of the house next door and walk all the way down to 60th Street and look out over the wonderful empty lot in which we played almost daily.

I keep going back every few years to keep tabs on 6044. I don't know how our old house will fare. Will it continue to go downhill or come back to what it once was? Tune in next century!

Me, John, Jule, Dan and Ed. The last photograph of us taken together. 1945.

About the Author

Designer, inventor, raconteur and professional mugwump, Paul Hogan is an internationally acclaimed advocate for children's play. He has designed and built playgrounds throughout the U.S. from Philadelphia to Hollywood and around the world from St. Petersburg, Russia to Port Morseby, Papua New Guinea. A tireless advocate for safe playgrounds, Hogan invented the MAX series of testing instruments. In 1979, President Carter appointed Hogan an Honorary Commissioner of the International Year of the Child. He received his B.A. at age 50 from Goddard College.

About the Cover

Front cover photograph courtesy of Temple University Urban Archives, Philadelphia, Pennslyvania.

Back cover photograph of Paul Hogan with his grandson, Colin Paul Tareila, by Paula Hogan.

Cover Design by Jerry Litofsky.